To my Survivor Friends
Especially

MMN

MomBj

&

Gen

LEARNING HOW TO REACH
SHREDDED
GRACE:
REACHING HIGHER

LEARNING HOW...VOLUME 5

Ann T. Ning Tan
&
FRIENDS

Table of Contents

LEARNING HOW is a NonProfit Corporation
www.shreddedgrace.com
@shreddedgrace

Ch. 1. Introduction – Welcome to the Club
MARLENE

YOU DIDN'T DIE.

WHAT DO YOU DO NOW?

At first I made a mock-up of this book cover with "You didn't die," as a joke. I was planning to go with the less inflammatory statement, "You lived."

But my "focus group" LOVED "You didn't die." Side note: they also decreed very loudly that I could not do the casual "looking away" pose for this cover, I hadto look directly at the camera. Boooo. PS Thanks for tolerating me, you guys.

And then I remembered that "You didn't die," is actually a direct quote from my sweet mother. It was early July 2011 – after I had flown from the hospital in Portland, OR, to the house I grew up in in Maryland. That flight took a lot out of me – it took more than a month for me to recover. Before I left inpatient (the 3rd and last hospital was RIO – The Rehabilitation Institute of Oregon) my longsuffering PT, Andrew, made sure I could walk the RIO loop (320+ ft) using a platform walker. After that flight I was intent on testing my physical abilities so I wouldn't lose ground while my outpatient schedule was being determined. However, I was grieved to find that I couldn't make it even 10 feet with a walker. (The hallway next to the kitchen is 10 feet.)

During one particularly discouraging attempt my Daddy brought me my wheelchair after about 3 feet because I was clearly fading and no one wanted to see me crumpled up on the floor. I cried and cried and told Mommy, *It would have been better if I had died.*

Side note: I never apologized to Mommy for saying that until January 2018. She said it was ok and that it was a natural way to think given what happened.

At the time, however, Mommy indicated that this train of thought was not going to be tolerated and pointed out,

Well, you DIDN'T DIE.

Mommy: [drops mic]

Me: *sniff sniff, blink blink*

She's a smart woman, unfailingly loving, and super tough. It is a formidable combination, I assure you. I mean, poor Daddy is a Very Scary Lawyer – the kind who will pretend not to notice anything and then all of a sudden you find yourself up the river without a paddle. But it's actually Mommy people should be worrying about. Not even kidding.

On my last day of inpatient, my hilarious OT, who was in charge of helping me get dressed, shook her head at the outfit my mother had chosen for me to wear on the airplane. Mommy had told me, YOU HAVE NO CLOTHES. Actually, I had a lot of clothes – but they were all on the Washington, D.C. formal side of business-casual, and I had very few rehab-appropriate items. So she chose what was familiar – I was almost always wearing a pink polo when not in the office. And during the colder months this became a long-sleeved pink striped oxford shirt. This is what she chose for me. Oxford shirts have a lot of buttons. So after I struggled for a while my OT said simply, *So....I'm going to help you now bc your Mom is going to be here in 2 minutes and say, THAT's NOT GOOD ENOUGH.*

LOL. My dear Mommy had *never* said anything to the staff except, Thank you for taking care of my daughter. But they all knew by the way she cared for me (lifting, helping to dress, grooming, etc.) that she is a force to be reckoned with.

Some of my first words were goal-oriented. Boo Boo (my sister) wrote about them on Facebook and I found them a year later when I wrote my first book. She had come to visit me at the 2nd Hospital (VIBRA) and I had told her in my raspy whisper, "I want to get off the Doctor's watch and on to *MOMMY's* watch."

And then I found out that Mommy's watch is actually A LOT stricter than hospital-based care.

When she told me, "Well, you DIDN't die," her implication was, *Well, what are you going to do about it?*

In a way, the answer to that question was a lot easier for me to get my mind around than the experience of many of my Survivor Friends. I had a clean break – it was obvious that I was unable to work, I moved across the country, and I had no family to care for. I could devote 100% of my resources to my own recovery. Whereas my friends have struggled with finishing school, finding a way to go back to work, and/or learning how to raise a child and run a household from a wheelchair, I was free to learn as much as possible and to have Mommy and Daddy pick up the slack.

Thanks, Mom and Dad! Xoxo

Example: Learning to walk is not a one-and-done deal. It took me YEARS to build the stamina and skills to do household tasks on my feet. I knew enough from other Survivors to understand that many were able to do way more than I could while in their wheelchairs. So I campaigned heavily for one. I did all my research and presented my proposal to my parents. I mean, come on – I am an adult. Thank God I had savings from before I got sick. If I want to spend money on a wheelchair, that's my decision, right?

WRONG.

When I asked Mommy she said, *Absolutely not.* And Daddy put on his scariest lawyer face at the mere mention of it. They were like, we will NOT be allowing another wheelchair to come into our home. You will learn to wash the dishes and do the laundry *on your feet, even if it takes longer than it would from a wheelchair.*

Hey, Mommy – thanks for all the extra work you did.

Side note: Eventually my parents relented, but AFTER I learned to do housework while standing.

Anyway, my friends have not had that luxury. I'm thinking of one friend in particular – **Marlene.**

I realized I mentioned her near the end of Randy's book, and in a podcast, but I didn't get the details of her story right, so here goes.

Marlene was 4 months pregnant with her first child when something exploded in her head on March 29, 2010. It was a Cavernous Malformation in her brainstem. Nobody knew it had been growing there until it exploded – it "hid out undetected, waiting for

11

the moment to ruin [her] life." Thankfully, she was at home with her husband, Stephen, who was able to get her to the hospital. The local neurosurgeon, however, declined to operate on a pregnant woman. Since she had not died the Cav Mal was simply deemed "inoperable." Marlene's only option was to do rehab for 3 weeks. It was later discovered, after her mom noticed some worsening physical symptoms and they did another MRI, that the raspberry-shaped abnormality in Marlene's brainstem was bleeding the whole time.

[GULP. I don't think you need to have had a brain bleed to understand that 3 weeks of continuous leakage is a Bad Thing.]

During that time, Marlene's family researched intervention options and she eventually traveled to the Barrow Clinic in Arizona for surgery. Marlene went into labor the day after, but they managed to delay the birth until almost full-term, and Marlene and Stephen welcomed their son, Nolan.

So Marlene figured out how to be disabled and care for a newborn at the same time. Thankfully, the little family lived with Marlene's mother for the first year so she could help out. In the early days Marlene could stand better than she can now. She seriously told me with zero trace of self-pity and superb matter-of-factness that this is how you can transport a baby from point A to point B: *You put him in the stroller, and if you lose your balance while pushing it, the rule is "HAND's OFF." This way, you will fall, but the baby is safe.*

She later explained that she chose to sit in her wheelchair more bc it was the safest way to care for Nolan. And bc her Cavernous Malformation was so *very much* in her brainstem, they couldn't get it all the first time around. She kept on having mini bleeds for around 4 years.

She first contacted me in 2013 bc she found me on Pinterest. I was blogging a lot then, and had posted some cheeky musings on Kelly Starret's *Becoming a Supple Leopard*. Marlene was like, *Ummm…can you run?*

Of course not, I answered. But now I can. (See *Learning How to Run (vol. 3) – Life is my Sport – with Randy Rocha*)

We lost touch and eventually the doctors explained to her, you will keep on bleeding and losing functionality until you have nothing else to lose unless we go in again. And so Marlene had her second surgery in January 2014, after which she lost everything again and spent a month in bed looking up at the ceiling bc her vision was so strange.

FYI, that looking at the ceiling thing is not uncommon. And sometimes your eyes are being so unruly you just shut them entirely bc the ceiling is doing weird things and it's just easier if you see nothing.

So, that's right – Marlene survived 2 brain surgeries. We reconnected in January 2017 and by November 2017 I convinced her to let me do a project with her. She had asked me the question,

"What is necessary for Recovery?"

This book, the podcasts and the videos (@shreddedgrace) are a really long answer to that question. I feel ready to tackle it because I realized that I've learned a LOT during these past (almost) 7 years of Recovery with spectacular results.

The fact that I lived has been referred to as "miraculous" by many, but for the first time this summer someone invoked the M-word specifically as it regards my Recovery. This person had not seen me in a couple years and was shocked (in a good way) at my progress. I received a lot of additional confirmation just within the past month that I have come a long way (understatement).

Multiple people who saw me before I met David and Randy, before I really hit my stride as a Survivor, have seen me recently and asked me, "HOW DID THIS HAPPEN?"

This book answers that question. It's a Survivorship 101 sort of handbook. I am often approached by Survivors of extreme medical trauma and/or violent crime. To be clear, I'm not *inviting* you to share your stories with me, necessarily, but I understand that I've opened myself to the possibility by building an online presence and writing/speaking in public. And if a person chooses to share his/her story with me I tell them, *thank you* for telling me that. And I mean it – bc I know from experience that it costs you something to admit that happened to you. Every time you have to say it out loud it hurts. But if you have the guts to tell me about it I won't flinch bc I know my job is to not make you more uncomfortable than you already are. It's a big deal to even verbalize it in the first place. But just bc I don't melt into a puddle right in front of you doesn't mean that you didn't just break my heart.

However, most people who approach me (strangers in the airport, restaurants, grocery store) have no idea what I do, they just see that I bear visible signs of trauma in my body and they follow their gut instinct to break normal social boundaries and tell me the sad things that have happened to them.

When Decision Day (see ch. 2) happened I knew immediately that I had to write and speak about Survivorship and Recovery. It has been amazing but kind of rough. In my defense, I had no idea what this would be like when I got sick. I don't think *anyone* can truly anticipate any number of life-events, but certainly not one like *this*. The thing is, people had more than a month of adjustment time while I was "asleep" (I also refer to this time as The Valley). When I woke up I did not understand anything bc nothing felt different in my head. The life I knew seemed like yesterday – there was no mental time lapse for me. I did not believe any of them when they said it was June. I insisted it was March and conceded *nothing*.

That month+ of The Valley was critical for the people surrounding me. During that time they digested the severity of my situation and understood that this meant I would be disabled for life. I had no such notion. Like I said, I conceded NOTHING.

And after I moved on from the acute stage of illness and embarked on the long road of medically stable Recovery I realized that even though I lost everything, the machinery of life still kept on moving without me. People have kids, get new jobs, move to new cities, and DO LIFE. It took me a while to understand that the experiences the majority of my peers have enjoyed as a matter of course as part of the natural ebb and flow of life will not be mine.

But I also learned that the fact that I got sick gained me entrance into a very exclusive club. And I was THRILLED to understand that even though it's very exclusive – membership is determined based on the fact that you survived a cataclysmic medical event and/or were the victim of a violent crime – I am NOT the only one out there. *(Side note: This is obviously not a club anyone <u>wants</u> to join. I'm just saying that if you happen to find yourself here, settle in and make yourself at home.)* I felt *so much* better when I realized that I was not alone.

Matt Hankey taught me this. He's my Survivor Friend with the orange and black logo of him looking fantastic in silhouette on his skateboard. He survived an AVM rupture when he was 16 in 2012. I badgered him into letting me work with him over a period of 6-12 months. Never mind that I have to Google almost everything he says bc he's so much younger than I am. We understand each other.

Once I told him some stuff about The Valley – stuff that I remembered but wished I could forget, stuff that I felt guilty about – stuff that I actually *missed*. He wrote to me, *I remember, too. Don't feel guilty. You're not the only one.*

SNIFF. That kid drives me nuts. (I know that technically he's not a kid, I just call him one.)

It was such a gift to me to hear Matt say, "You're not the only one." He verbalized simply, *you are not alone*. So I set out to prove to him, *Yeah? Well, you're not alone, EITHER.* And we launched the original Shredded Grace – and I found Diahanne the

Pool Ninja to train him, and rallied the troops to "Help Matt Walk Again."

With the advent of Marlene, however, Shredded Grace became bigger than either one of us. Matt is making phenomenal progress with Diahanne. Life is opening up for him because he is finally getting to answer the question, *Will I walk again?* And when I told Matt I had a new Survivor friend he immediately signed on to encourage Marlene. Matt is living proof that Recovery can happen even after hope has stalled and you're wondering if you'll ever get a chance to get better.

The verb "to shred" means to improvise at a high level of proficiency on a skateboard, or on a guitar. I TOTALLY just made that definition up in my head based on a conversation with Coach R, and an old vid Matt's friend took of the kids at the skate park. It was an interview style clip, and they asked a child, *What do you think about what happened to Matt?*

And the child, who is probably a young man now, said simply, *BAD. I want him to SKATE!! I want him to come SHRED with us!!*

I love that vid. But I did not understand this word, "shred." So of course I immediately consulted Coach Randy, who explained it to me in both skateboarding terms and also in the more general usage – as an adjective, e.g. if you say someone is "shredded" you mean they are intensely muscular.

So when I chose the name "Shredded Grace," it's a nod to skateboarding but I'm really using it in the "intensely muscular" sense. And I put "Grace" in there because *Grace* is something you don't deserve.

It was not my right to walk again, it is my privilege. It is a privilege not granted to everyone. But I was made to understand from the beginning that I was not paralyzed and the nature of my injury meant that I had the opportunity to pursue mobility. So I did. And this book is to encourage Marlene, and other Survivors, who are asking the question, is it worth it?

Short answer: YES.

We are going to do some nitty gritty how-to's of Survivor life, e.g. How to make and use a Medical Resume, and some more high level stuff – Behaviors of Successful Survivorship – e.g. how to find HELP, and how to Cultivate Survivor GRIT. And I have gotten my Survivor Friends to help me with the heavy lifting. Making this a Team efforts was intentional. The message here is that we are not alone – we learn from each other. It's just because I like to write that I'm the one aggregating this information. And in the event that you are not a Survivor yourself, it is highly likely that at some point you will have a loved one who is. So this book still merits reading bc it will help you be a better advocate. However, I maintain that *everyone* is surviving *something*. But I'm also told that my writing voice is just fun, so even if you have absolutely zero interest in Survivorship and Recovery, please stick around to be entertained.

However, before we proceed, I'd like to address Survivors specifically:

If you are reading this book from your hospital bed, let me welcome you to RecoveryLand and just say that the fact that you are able to read is quite a triumph. And the fact that you are already thinking about what to do next is a good sign. You will never reach your potential unless you decide to act in the first place.

You *cannot* **succeed**
unless you **begin**.

If your eyes are problematic and you have used up all of your visual capital, please proceed to YouTube. You may also follow me in general on social media @shreddedgrace. I will also be posting a gallery of pics that correspond to the chapters in this book at www.shreddedgrace.com

5 Ground Rules for Survivors:

1. DO NOT COMPARE: We are not comparing levels of trauma, how much we have suffered, or the nature of our Recoveries. I did not understand this when I woke up. I was just EXTREMELY unhappy that the guy who had a stroke last week was going home before me. Seriously? They said I had a stroke, too. Whatever. Comparing, and you probably *are* comparing bc you are likely researching treatment options online, will discourage you if you say to yourself, *Why can't my experience be like THAT?* You are doing your homework now by reading this book or watching the videos so that you are better equipped to go write your *own* story.

2. DO NOT ELOPE: To "elope" is to escape from the hospital. Please do not attempt it. They will catch you, and there will be consequences. They know how to look out for people like us, and then after you've proven yourself to be a troublemaker through your misguided bid for freedom, they will keep an even closer watch on you. Trying to escape is not an uncommon behavior. One of my hospitals keeps a large 3-ring binder at the front desk called "The Elopement Log." I was like, do you seriously need a binder that big? Yeah, they do. Every day people try to wheel

or shuffle out of the front doors. The only successful story of elopement I've heard of was of an older gentleman who was so confused and so intent on going home that he ripped his tracking bracelet off his wrist and wheeled his chair 8 miles to his home. It was his wife who turned him in bc she had found him sitting outside, knocking pathetically on the window.

I am not condoning this behavior. But 8 miles?!?! Sir, I congratulate you on your scrappiness.

3. EXPRESS APPRECIATION and AWARENESS: One of my CNA's told Mommy about me, *She says 'thank you.' We are not used to that.* Most people in the rehab hospital are not happy to be there – they got sick in a life-altering way after all, and they take it out on the staff. Apparently yelling and throwing things is common. Set yourself apart by being grateful for the care you receive and if you can talk, by expressing it. I understood early on that people were being kind to me – they were VERY kind (sniff sniff sniff) when I was at my most vulnerable. And so I thanked them. This made them even more committed to my care.

The flip side to this is that we all know that bad things can happen and if you're alone in the hospital you can be an especially easy target.

The Lord protected me from harm throughout my inpatient life, and it really helped that Mommy and Daddy were extremely visible and my friends from church sent a clear signal: *there are a lot of people watching, and we care about how she is treated.*

If your loved one cannot communicate it is CRUCIAL that friends and family make their presence known in the hospital. I will talk about this more in ch. 14 "What to do if Someone You Love is "Asleep" in the hospital. Mommy told a hospital administrator once, *She cannot speak for herself. She cannot do ANYTHING for herself. If she were your daughter, what would you do?*

Mommy (and Daddy) made sure I had top-notch care, that's what they did. My siblings made their presence known via constant phone calls. And there was a steady stream of visitors (once I made it out of the ICU) that told everyone that my situation was being monitored closely.

Even though I know in retrospect that the people around me demanded the highest level of care for me and the hospital staffs rose to the occasion, I still shiver when I remember the sensation of being unable to do anything but watch as things I did not understand happened to me. There was a lot of mental self-talk like, *This isn't happening, this isn't happening* (incorrect – it actually WAS happening), and *No, no, PLEASE no.* (impassioned, but ineffectual since I could not move or speak).

But as soon as I was able to express any kind of awareness, I did so. I asked questions like, *Why are you taking my blood?* I actually didn't care – I just wanted them to know that I was awake enough to understand what was going on and that it was still my body and I fully intended to decide what happened. Granted, when I started doing this I did not believe that this had really happened. I just figured that even if I were stuck in this horrible dream it still behooved me to look after my own interests.

4. LEARN: I know, I know. You're probably annoyed at all your Therapists. Oh, wait – that was just me? Sorry, my bad. I was annoyed bc I saw no reason for me to be there. I thought the story about the Brain Bleed was absolutely preposterous and I did not know I could not walk. They must have thought it would have been self-evident, but I was so loopy, and in my moments of coherent thought I still conceded nothing. I looked around at my Medical Team like, *Umm.......I don't think you understand what's going on here – I am a VERY high functioning adult. Cognitively, I could run*

circles around you any day. INCLUDING TODAY.

Sorry I'm so mean. But the point is that once I admitted that I did not know how to live within this new set of physical parameters, and I recognized that the professionals around me had special knowledge I needed, I decided to learn what I could from them, I actually started to make progress.

5. KEEP THE WALKER ON THE FLOOR: This is a quote from Andrew, PT2, the one who survived The Wall incident (see David's book – vol. 2 – *Learning How to Live*) At first I was like, *AHEM. Let me get this straight: You – a completely able bodied person – wish to boss me around regarding how to use this stupid thing? If we come to a corner I will pick that walker up off the ground if I FEEL LIKE IT (Insert emoji with slit eyes).* Sorry, Andrew. For the record, Andrew was super nice to me and super smart. He put up with a lot. They all do. Ask David and Randy. Anyway, Andrew was trying to teach me walker and wheelchair basics so I could leave the hospital since I had already been very vocal that the goal was to get me travel-ready *stat*. I'm including this as a ground rule so you know that the basics did not come to me intuitively. They were learned behaviors that have kept me safe. So don't just roll your

eyes like I did. Try it their way. It will be better for everyone.

Okay, the ground rules are over. Now let's move on. We have to start at Square One:

IS IT OKAY THAT YOU LIVED?

PS. I forgot to tell you: None of this is intended to be medical advice. Please seek out medical professionals you can trust and be guided by their expertise. However, you are the steward of your own health. You are responsible for knowing the details of what happened, making sure your Team is informed, seeking out your options, and making the final decision. Carol Ridgely taught me that (*Vol. 4- Learning How to Sing a New Song*). She never verbalized it, I just watched her do it for do it for 15 years. And when I got sick I knew that victory in illness is possible because of her.

But just so we're clear:

I AM **NOT** A DOCTOR. THESE ARE MY CREDENTIALS:

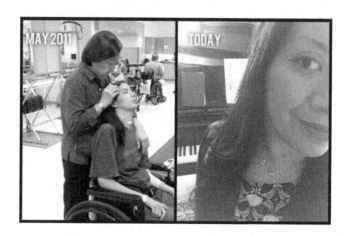

WAYS TO ENGAGE:

- ShreddedGrace.com →Media
    - o **Videos** – episode gallery
    - o **Pictures** – organized according to chapter
    - o **The Shredded Grace Podcast** – available on iTunes and at Podbean.com
    - o **Blog** - "Learning How"
    - o **Instagram** @shreddedgrace
- **Youtube** @shreddedgrace
- **Amazon.com** – all Learning How books are non profit – Search: *Ann T. Ning Tan*

Ch. 2 Is it Ok that you lived?
Decision Day - Ruth

"Is it okay that you lived, Ning?"

I had literally JUST met Ruth ten minutes earlier, and she just asked me that question with ZERO hesitation – just a kind smile and sweet voice that told me she knew *exactly* what she was doing and had been planning this moment for a while.

Ruth is the ONLY person on the face of this planet who is qualified to ask me that question. It's THE QUESTION – the one that only *you* can answer, and the one you must settle on before the work of Recovery can begin.

I just said that only YOU are the one who can decide if it's *okay that you lived*. But because Ruth asked me this question, I like to ask other people. I cannot answer it for you, but I can tell you my experience.

If you want peace to accept that your past (no matter how sheltered or shattered) is a part of who you are and the power to become the person you were meant to be, there is only one solution for you: Jesus Christ.

I was going to be a missionary. I visited Burundi in March 2011 and had been invited by the believers there to relocate permanently as a missionary/financial analyst (that was my pre-AVM profession). I was THRILLED that God would choose *me* for such an honorable service. There is an established work in Burundi, with a ton of health and education ministries that show people that God loves them in practical ways. When I visited I sometimes caught a whiff of the history of violence the Burundians grew up with. What was accepted as commonplace (they had ALL experienced these things) made me shudder. War had shaped a generation – I saw suffering, I saw grief, I saw great sorrow – but I also saw hope.

Side note: *Google "Carl Johnson, Burundi"* *for more info*

I returned to the States full of this hope, ready to set sail after over a year of intense spiritual preparation and seeking. I flew back to Oregon and four days prior to the meeting I had scheduled to ask my Oregon Church to send me to Africa, something exploded in my brain and left me for dead.

I woke up over a month later with some weird physical sensations (everything was literally spinning – I could even feel it when I was lying flat on my back with my eyes closed) but cognitively I felt no difference and no time lapse. As I regained consciousness I tried to construct a plausible reason for the things going on around me. When my "Train circling Portland at high speed" and my "Really bad Reality TV Show" Theories were both rejected, I decided to REFUSE to believe this absolutely ridiculous AVM thing had actually occurred and insisted that this was all a

29

dream – none of this was actually happening bc I said, *There is NO WAY God would have let this happen to me.*

Spoiler alert: There was a way.

Ruth was uniquely qualified to ask me "Is it ok that you lived?" bc she is the mother of Joy Johnson – The Johnsons are the missionary family I visited in Burundi prior to my AVM Rupture. When I was in The Valley I dreamed of being at their house, and going to language school in preparation for my move to Africa. Ruth is a missionary, too – she and her husband, Brian, were serving in Ethiopa with their two daughters. Ruth was in a car going out to do some counseling in the bush when they were hit head-on by a coffee been truck.

Ruth was the most seriously injured in the wreck. She had to lie on the ground overnight while they waited for transportation back to the capital. She knew it was bad – she touched her leg and couldn't feel anything. A colleague sat next to Ruth that night and predicted her she would live and would tell this story in years to come.

She told ME her story. I am only one of the people blessed by her testimony, but now you are, too. But, as Ruth says herself – this story is His. *May His name be glorified.*

Ruth and Brian's family had to move back to America where they learned how to serve Stateside and navigate This Disabled Life. Ruth was paralyzed from the chest down. There are a *lot* of crazy hardcore things she has dealt with to learn how to live like this, and Brian, and the rest of the family learned, too. When I got sick word traveled fast. Ruth lives near Chez Boo Boo. The first Sunday after my AVM Rupture my sister's family went to church. Ruth and Brian were there. She put her arms around Boo Boo's neck and squeezed – *I just wanted to come give you a hug.*

SNIFF. Thanks for doing that, Ruth.

A couple of years later I was visiting Boo Boo and she took me to Ruth' s house. That's when Ruth asked me THE QUESTION.

Survivorship gives you the liberty to cut to the chase. My friend, KRK, refers to visible signs of physical trauma as "instant credibility." But it wasn't just the fact that Ruth was in a power chair that made me want to listen to her - it was the context of her own injury, and her gentle demeanor that the Lord used to touch my heart that day.

Thankfully, I had already decided that it IS okay that I lived. This is my story:

I woke up still able to exercise my powers of logic. In fact, that was one of the only things I *could* do while bedridden. I can put two and two together. I knew that if it were true that God had put me in a wheelchair instead of sending me to Africa it had *very serious* implications for my faith. I was unprepared to deal with this issue as an inpatient. It was too much, mentally. Besides – I was busy devoting my waking moments to figuring out how to escape the notice of Andrew, my LSPT (long-suffering Physical Therapist) long enough to harm myself badly enough to allow me to just escape entirely from this situation.

Yes, that is code for Suicide. I will speak very plainly – I was VERY angry. I have pointed out before that it was God's grace that made me so acutely disabled in the beginning that all I could do was lie there. When they taught me to sit, or at least lie on an incline, I literally had to devote 100% of my faculties to the act of breathing. It was awful. And terrifying – bc if I lost concentration for a moment I'd panic bc of the interruption to my air supply. But eventually I didn't have to think so much about breathing, and then I just thought about how awful this whole situation was – and then I didn't want to deal with it.

So I *insisted* that I was stuck in a very bad dream. I collected mental notes on what everyone said, I asked everyone "quiz" questions to prove their reality, I started verbally pushing the staff at RIO (3ʳᵈ Hospital) upstairs (where inpatients live) and downstairs (where we get Therapy) to get them to admit that this entire thing was a farce and they were all figments of my imagination. They were kind nurses, CNA's, techs, and Therapists. I got the feeling that my level of confusion and the manner in which I presented it were not the usual level of patient-discomfort they dealt with. But they met me with kindness and did what they could. The bottom line is that I would come away from these interactions disappointed. I couldn't get anyone to agree with me – but I always tried again the next day.

This behavior continued throughout the rest of my inpatient career and about a month after I got discharged. When I got out of the hospital and flew with MommyDaddy from Portland, OR to the D.C. area I was pleased to be back in familiar surroundings – but there was no getting around the fact that I had to learn to navigate them in a wheelchair. I slept downstairs and had a baby monitor. I was not allowed to transfer in or out of bed solo, although I had been trained to do so, but my parents were still on high alert and wouldn't allow it. In their defense, I think I did look rather glassy-eyed and I can tell from some pics that something weird was going on with my torso. I held it in a way that indicated I had no trunk control. So I don't blame my parents for not letting me do stuff.

The thing is, though, that I did it anyway. God mercifully preserved me from harm and so many years have passed that I can write about it and not get in trouble. I chafed under the restrictions of my new situation. I had mandatory Nap Time – which I absolutely needed bc the transition out of being bedridden is rough. (*Side note: Nap Time is no longer mandatory – I've just accepted that I need it. E.g. while writing this book I got in bed to rest "just for a few minutes" at 9am. Yes, that is usually the time of my first nap. I woke up 4 hours later. Oops. It's amazing that I get anything done at all.*) But early on I was so annoyed I would totally roll out of my bed, lower myself down to the floor, and crawl around the room and look at stuff. There were plenty of books (I slept downstairs in the "Library" – but it's really where there's a TV and Daddy's computer), and a phone. Sadly, my parents had changed the phone system since I moved and I didn't know how to work it. I was trying to call my sister one day while I was supposed to be sleeping and inadvertently dialed 911. Oops. The operator was SO NICE. I told him I had made a mistake and he said, *That's okay – thanks for staying on the line to tell me!*

And one night Mommy left my wheelchair close enough to my bed that I transferred back into it at 1am. Usually she wheeled my chair several feet away, and I knew from experience that I was unable to crawl to my chair and hoist myself up into it, so that night I waited a reasonable amount of time for her and Daddy to fall asleep, and then I went JOY RIDING. I just went to the kitchen and ate some Froot Loops. But I assure you that it was a kitchen mobility triumph

– I got my bowl and spoon, the milk, my cereal – everything by myself and then crunched away as I reflected darkly on how much I hated all of this. And when I was done I put everything away so Mommy would never know.

Things came to a critical point, however, by July. This is an excerpt from Vol. 1 Learning How...ch. 10 "The Turning Point"

In my mind, death would have been preferable. At least it would have been a lot easier than all this recovery! Dying would have been easy for me – I'm ready, and there was no pain since I passed out. It's the business of living that's hard. As my mother sagely pointed out, though, it's a fact that death would have been easier for me, but that's not the reality of what happened that day. My surgeon did his job really well, and here I am, hobbling along with my cane and writing this account for typing practice.

It's true that this situation could be much worse. I've seen daily proof of that at the rehab hospitals. My point is that this is bad enough as it is. I will never forget crawling to my wheelchair and then sobbing out of frustration. These days I remind myself that I know some folks who would be grateful to be able to crawl, and that God has given me peace about this situation. This is not to say that I'm not deeply sad about it, though. One day I tore a bunch of heart-shaped sticky notes in half and posted them on my bedroom wall to signify my broken heart. I still reach out in the dark and touch them from my bed. I know, though, that Christ came to heal the broken-hearted, and I have hope.

I wasn't always this hopeful. In fact, when I first came home I adopted a "whatever works" attitude, meaning that I would do whatever made me better and discard what didn't, including my faith. I had been four days away from asking my church's permission to move to Africa as a missionary, and then my brain bled. I woke up and everything was gone, including my job, my apartment, many of my motor skills, and my ability to walk. One day at mealtime I was so discouraged by the way I ate that I told Mom that I was like an animal. Those days in the hospital were hard, and so were the days at home.

One morning in late July I was lying in my bed, waiting for Mom to come get me and ruminating over my plight. In those days I gave my mom a status update first thing in the morning. "It hasn't happened yet," I would tell her, "it" being the overnight healing I fully expected. It hurt my feelings terribly to read the Gospels with Dad. We'd read out loud to exercise my voice and feed my soul. I read several accounts of how Christ healed people left and right, and I knew my ailments were nothing to Him, so I wondered why He didn't do something that wouldn't cost Him any effort.

"I would never have chosen this," I thought to myself that morning as I waited for Mom. And then the following thought imprinted itself on my mind: "He chose this." I was astounded to think that as drastic as I thought my situation was, He chose to submit Himself to limitations infinitely more severe. Those 33 years must have offended His senses in every way, but He chose to live and die for love. I had been planning to ask my friend, Anthony, what had convinced him to convert to Christianity as an adult, but after this morning meditation, all my questions were answered, and the buzzing in my head became quiet.

I couldn't argue with what happened at the cross, nor could I take issue with Christ's own commentary about it. The problem is that His claims to deity and exclusivity are things that nice people would never say. I knew I couldn't pick and choose what I liked about Christianity and ignore the things that made me uncomfortable. The bottom line was that "He chose this," and despite my stroke and the craziness that ensued, that thought settled all my questions and keeps me going every day.

I refer to this day, July 24, 2011, as Decision Day – the day I decided that the Gospel is true, i.e. Jesus Christ's claims about Himself are true. I decided on that day that I could still believe what I had believed prior to my injury even though something really bad happened to me.

A few things:
- My decision was based on publicly available information and ordinary logic
- I received ZERO Special Knowledge in the Valley of the Shadow of Death – no divine revelation, no shining angels talking to me, NOTHING. At first I thought I got jipped, but…
- I am not asking anyone to take my word for

what I saw, or what I learned as a result of my near-death experience

- I AM telling you what happened to me, and am pointing out that if I evaluated the claims of Christ and found them to be compelling and ultimately true even though I have been given a set of extreme circumstances, these claims at least merit your own examination

I also hasten to point out that I do not have the answer to everything. But just bc I can't explain everything doesn't mean it's not true. The bottom line is that Jesus Christ met the need of my heart and it was a DEEP need.

I wrote this blog post below in response to a question posed online in a public forum. I had avoided engaging in this group discussion for months, but one morning the talk got SO intense that it was clear that this person was in very deep trouble. So I rolled my sleeves up like, *FINE. Let's just DO THIS.* As soon as Decision Day happened I knew what I'd have to do. So I set about building an online presence that A) gives me a place to talk about Jesus Christ B) allows Survivors to choose their own level of engagement. My beliefs are *mine.* I'm not saying all of the friends who have been so gracious to let me write about them believe the same thing as I do, because they don't – so please don't blame them for any of my crazy. Similar to how I like people to opt-in to help me, I like the people who contact me for Survivor

Reasons to opt-in to hearing what I have to say about Jesus Christ. I know it's not the normal stuff you hear about how Christ was a good teacher and challenged us to live above the norm and become our best selves.

That's true – I'm not sniffing at it, but in an exercise of intellectual authenticity I am obligated to recognize the fact that not only was Christ a good moral teacher, He also claimed to be God Himself. He also claimed to be the One Way. These facts are not hidden knowledge – most Bibles print Christ's words in red ink – but they are not often talked about bc it is more socially palatable to concentrate on the Good Teacher idea.

So, yeah – I realize I just talked about a topic that most people would not like to discuss. The thing is, it's what saved me from a lifetime of Anger and Bitterness, so it's not like I'm gonna sit here and NOT TELL YOU. *Especially* if I know you're in trouble. So I wrote back to that person (in the group forum) and said, *Hey, I know the answer to this – but it involves Jesus Christ. If you want to know more [click on this link] – it goes to my personal blog.* I like to make people choose to engage – you click on the link if you want to know more. I pay for that piece of the internet with my own money. I am ABSOLUTELY not going to shove anything down your throat – I know better than anyone that if a Survivor is not ready to talk, you should respect that. So I like people to choose to read my stuff. Other people besides that person read this blog post. And although these people do not believe the same things as I do I received kind messages saying, Thank You for tackling this.

165. How to Get a Heart Transplant
blog.annninglearninghow.com
published May 7, 2013

Okay, I'm gonna get all **crazy** on you and just **call a spade a spade** because I have encountered some situations lately where people are just absolutely miserable, and I know that kind of misery – you feel like a gutted fish and wish so desperately to have a different set of circumstances. Better, preferably, but different will do – because living the way you are is unbearable. There is only so much talking about professional help and different life-coaching techniques one can talk about. I'm not knocking these concepts, (I've actually found some helpful) I'm just saying that they can only take you so far. If you want true and lasting transformation…if you want peace to accept that your past (no matter how sheltered or shattered) is a part of who you are and the power to become the person you were meant to be, there is only one solution for you: Jesus Christ.

Oooh – I said It. I said The Name. It's a divisive Name these days – but it's also "the Name which is above every name…." and as I told M (37) the first time she confiscated my cane, "ran" me around the hospital, and then let me retrieve Leo, "Thank the Lord…and I do *not* talk about the Lord lightly." I've given you the punchline, so you can opt out now if you want to. One more thing – the word "transplant" is in quotation marks in my title since I am not talking about a physical organ transplant. If you are looking for information on getting a transplant I'm sure there are a gazillion web resources for you. A couple of dear ones in my life have received organs from others and let me just take a moment to encourage you to **become an organ donor** if you don't already have the little heart on your license. And if you're waiting for a transplant or recovering from one, <3.

On to business: Have you ever been so miserable you can't get out of bed in the morning? Not being able to get out of bed is a relatively mild manifestation of the misery I am referring to. I have referenced how God answered my questions before, but I'm not sure if I've ever spelled it out. So here goes.

I was miserable when we flew home. My mind was like a hamster on a wheel and the mental friction was making me so uncomfortable I feel like vomiting right now just thinking about it. Seriously, if God had not intervened for me my eyeballs would have popped out of their sockets from the stress. Sorry to be so graphic, but I don't know any other way to describe it – it was messy. It was a blessing that I was physically unable to take any meaningful action from my grief.

Thankfully, God knew I could not handle this kind of pressure for too long. When I say He "intervened" – I do not mean that I woke up one morning and there was cloud-writing in the sky that said, "I did not forget you – I did this on purpose and you can trust Me," although that would have been undeniably fabulous. But what is significant to me is that even though something really bad happened to me, God make me okay with it via completely ordinary, publicly available means.

I believe that Christ is the One Redemptive Solution for the world we live in. This is not new or privileged knowledge (at least where I live). I learned about this by reading and listening to things available through a simple Google search or going to a hotel and looking at the Bible in the nightstand etc. Then God gave me some extreme circumstances. Yes, they are extreme, but let me just say again that I'm grateful that **my condition did not arise** from an act of carelessness or violence on the part of another person. I have been spared that, but many are not. Anyway, my decision to keep on believing what I believed before I got sick was based on the fact that I decided to examine my beliefs and discard them if they didn't make sense to me (Spoiler Alert: My beliefs withstood the scrutiny and I kept them). There was no supernatural experience or heavenly vision – I was just lying in my bed (because I was unable to do anything else) and I *thought*.

So that's what saved me from a lifetime of anger and bitterness. I see lots of people with many reasons to be angry and bitter. These are reasons I don't take issue with – they would make me angry, too. But anger+bitterness just eats you alive like poison from the inside out. The problem is that the notion of pulling yourself up by your bootstraps, while immensely attractive in its appeal to the human desire to exert self-control, be a problem-solver, and determine your destiny, will not allow you change in a lasting way. You need a heart transplant. A complete transformation.

Perhaps you are not angry or bitter and never have
been. I'm glad you don't have to tussle with those
feelings, but the thing is that the One Redemptive
Solution is predicated on the notion that *need* is
universal. This is not about learning a new "strategy
for living" (as my friend F said, once) – strategies for
living are all over the place these days. This is about
life, period. Specifically, moving from death to life.
And the Solution that works under extreme
circumstances is the same one that functions when life
is relatively rosy and smooth. You're not aiming at a
moving target – it's stationary – but the idea is
that *everyone* has already missed the mark, and it
requires Divine intervention to have peace with God.

If you read until the end, thanks for hanging in there
with me. :).

Luke 4.18 "... he hath sent me to heal the
brokenhearted..."

Ch. 3 There's No Crying in Baseball
WHY WALKING IS SCARY AND WHY YOU SHOULD DO IT
ANYWAY

This chapter is for people who have the opportunity to walk again and are struggling with whether or not they should go for it. If you have a permanent or degenerative condition that excludes you from this category, please proceed to the next chapter.

Just kidding. You can read on if you want to, it's just that I have **major Survivor Guilt** over the fact that I get to walk again while others do not. *Sigh.* Yours is a hardcoreness I cannot speak to – but the fact that I was given the opportunity to pursue mobility means that I have emerged from this event with specific views on if one should try to learn to walk.

Short Answer: YES, you should try to learn to walk.

Some of you might be like, *Uh, WHY would a person not try to walk if they had the opportunity?* Answer: there are a lot of reasons. The biggest one I dealt with was simply FEAR. I'm talking, completely terror-stricken, sobbing in secret, nauseous all the time, *FEAR.*

I was mostly afraid of falling, still angry that I was now 100% dependent on another person, and terrified that I would cry in front of Andy Frankenstein.

I had formed the notion very early on in my consciousness that if you show ANY SIGN OF WEAKNESS in RecoveryLand, you will be summarily eaten for lunch by the wild animals prowling around the periphery (I live(d) in a constantly elevated state of Fight or Flight).

The solution to this, I told myself, is two-fold:

1) Never EVER Cry. Bc there is NO CRYING IN BASEBALL. Crying in secret is okay as long as no one ever sees you and these incidents are sporadic. Tears are an indulgence. Do not be a sissy.
2) Be MEAN. Expect nothing from anyone, and then you won't be disappointed.

So, ummmmm....is anyone really *surprised* that I'm in therapy? To be clear, these two ways of thinking are coping mechanisms I hit on soon early in my Recovery so I could Survive. We have moved on from Survival mode to Thriving and I understand now that this is an unhelpful and unhealthy way to think. Reprogramming these thought habits is really difficult, though.

So instead of addressing my specific areas of struggle, I'm going to address 4 Major Fears about Walking that will apply to the general mobility-pursuing population.

FEAR 1: You might Fall.

My AVM was primarily in the cerebellum – that's why my balance is so appalling. Falling is very scary if you have no way to correct yourself if you feel yourself losing your balance. In the beginning, however, I didn't feel myself losing it – it was a constant state of loss that I had to adjust to. It was so weird – I would just find myself on the ground all of a sudden. Having mobility problems just exacerbates the fear of falling bc a sprain, tear, or break will have a more significant impact on you than the general population since you already can't walk in the first place. So you sit there thinking, *What if I fall? Am I going to set myself back even more?*

Why you should do it anyway:

We should just get this out of the way. The issue is not that you *might* fall. I'm telling you right now that **YOU *WILL* FALL.** There is only one way to learn – experientially – I know, I checked.

So the number one step is to simply accept that you *will* be falling. But there is something you can do to mitigate the fear of falling:

<u>KNOW HOW TO FALL</u>

I have been taught two ways. Please note, I did not learn these techniques in Rehab. A Physical Therapist might have a different perspective. I learned A as a kid in gymnastics, and it's the mental technique I used to learn to walk. Let the record show that Andy Frankenstein NEVER let me fall. All the times I fell were in Real Life, or when I was in inpatient and was loopy and just tried to do stuff. But once I knew that falling hurt and that my balance was completely shot I made a contingency plan (A).

A. If you fall you automatically curl up into a ball and roll. Draw your limbs in – RESIST the temptation to put your hand out – if you do, something might snap.

B. Trainer D's method (based in BJJ). I declined to learn this bc this is not a good option for me given my arm motor skills. He then offered to teach me (assuming I had already fallen on the ground) that thing when you're on you're back and then suddenly snap back up to your feet using only momentum and no limbs whatsoever. I declined this, too. But the Falling Method is that when you hit the ground you roll, but you also slam a fist into the ground to absorb the shock.

FEAR 2: You have to trust someone else.

On my first day of Outpatient PT Andy Frankenstein made me stand on a mini trampoline that was positioned between two iron railings. I held on for dear life. He had a hardcore intern, so there were TWO people who were fully absorbed in my safety.

The task was just to stand there. Please remember: I had learned to hold my own head up only within the last two months. Standing was still new. I already felt like I lived in a washing machine on the spin cycle, so just feeling the instability of the trampoline was enough stimulation at that point. When Andy told me to climb off he sensed that I had no idea how to do so – and he simply put his hand out to help me.

I flatly refused. Not verbally – I just managed to disembark while maintaining a death grip on the bars. I was thinking, *Ummmm, I don't hold hands with random people. WHAT IS WRONG WITH YOU?!?!*

We had just met and I considered Andy Frankenstein to be a stranger. I was not amused by how everyone was holding my hand. It was even more galling when I admitted that I *needed* to hold someone's hand.

Everyone puts out a hand to help, BTW. When you see someone like me (at least how I moved in the early days), it's just instinct – flight attendants and custodians as well as Physical Therapists have dropped everything to hold my hand or do an instinctive full-body guard when they saw me approach. Actually, it wasn't just the early days. Workers in grocery stores still give me a wide berth and wait for me to pass before rolling through with their hand trucks and carts. One of them explained to Mommy, *I saw her face!* LOL.

Walking is a metaphor for life. Eventually you're gonna have to trust someone else. Yeah. I learned that the hard way. But now I know – Survivorship and Grit do NOT happen in a vacuum. I needed other people to show me how to do this. And now it's my duty to pass that information along.

A couple of thoughts:
 A. The people Rehabbing you are highly incentivized to *not* let you fall. Andy Frankenstein told me in typical AndyCode, "There's a lot of paperwork." Another PT was more candid: *I get in trouble if you fall. DON'T DO IT.*
 B. Not everyone out there is going to burn you. In fact, some of them might even keep you from falling even when (s)he is not acting in a professional capacity. This is also something you must learn experientially. It took me a Very Long time to start believing this.

FEAR 3: It's going to drain your resources.

My Recovery has been great bc I have had the liberty to devote all of my time, money, and energy to it. That was a conscious decision on my part, and I'm grateful to have been in the position at the time of my injury to have the resources to do this. Although I BEGGED God for an overnight miracle when I first got sick and still have zero trouble believing that He could do it for me no problem, I ascertained early on that this did not appear to be His will for me. Like Decision Day, He has brought about my healing via ordinary means that can be observed and verified by anyone. Translation: Recovery is A LOT of hard work. It will definitely drain your resources.

Why you should do it anyway:
If you have financial and social obligations that require your resources, Recovery might not be at the top of your priority list. But I contend that Recovery will add to your quality of life, increasing your earning potential, or at least making it less painful for you to hold a job in the long term, and as you heal you will have more bandwidth to be a functional, contributing member of your family and your community. Only you can decide what needs to come, 1st, 2nd, 3rd, however – your family's situation is unique and I will not presume to have insight into all of that. If you DO decide that Recovery should be prioritized, however – it's like anything else. You plan for it. You save money for it. You do it. And then you enjoy it.

FEAR 4: You might be unsuccessful.
Is the goal for you to walk again?

This is the type of question that only a Survivor can ask another Survivor. I posed this question to a nice young man during Pool Therapy. He had just eschewed the lift and catapulted himself directly from his wheelchair into the water using his upper body and the ladder. I was deeply impressed by this, and he had a gentle, friendly demeanor, so I decided to get nosey.

Yes – they said I will walk again. I was shot in the chest three times a couple years ago. That's why I'm in this chair. I wasn't living a good life back then. I was doing unhealthy, unsafe things. But now I have a daughter and I'm going to do better for her.

*Hmmm....*I thought to myself. *Shot in the chest 3x? You don't hear that every day. But I guess that's why he's wearing a t-shirt in the pool.* (Now I know this is not uncommon – a lot of us like to remain covered up so no one sees any scars.)

I met him several years ago. And I hope he's walking!! But here's the thing – people made predictions about me early on but I didn't believe them. I stopped believing anything anyone said about my physical condition (See Vol. 3 *Learning How to Run* Ch. 3 *"If you Want to Do this Right"*) bc I was afraid of failure.

Early on, a *very* experienced PT who did not treat me regularly, but was in a leadership position represented her department at a Rehab "Family Conference" my parents had called so everyone would report out on my progress. At this meeting, this PT said, *She's gonna walk in X weeks.* It was generally accepted that I *would* walk – lots of professionals had made comments in passing to this effect – they could tell just by the way I was moving my legs to help drive my wheelchair that I'd walk again. But this was the first time someone had attached a timeline to it.

Note: This PT was very well credentialed and had seen a vast sample of the patient population. Offering a timeline was not an unreasonable thing for her to do.

The deadline of X weeks came and went. I was not walking. The fear I felt deteriorated into despair. I had FAILED. Something was WRONG WITH ME.

Why you should do it anyway:
Eventually, I *did walk*, but it was later than foreseen. It is possible, however, that someone could set out with the intent to walk, but they are ultimately unsuccessful. However, I have not heard any stories of this scenario yet. In fact, the only scenarios I *have* heard of are when the doctors say, *you'll never walk again*, but the patient does, anyway.

But still, my mind is built to consider the Worst Case Scenario as very possible. And it stands to reason that people just don't tell stories about failed Mobility attempts. So, yes – let's assume that one of the outcomes could be that you are ultimately unsuccessful in your pursuit of Mobility.

DO IT ANYWAY.

You don't know for sure if you'll succeed or fail – there's only one way to find out.

A. If you do not even try you will always be plagued by the thought, *What if...?*
B. Someone is watching you – like that nice young man at the pool – he knew his daughter was going to watch him. Even if you try and *fail*, how you approach it is a valuable life-lesson you want your kids to see

PS. Ignore the timelines. And please do not give up too soon. (Coach R's wrestling advice: *Do not submit too early. Bonus tip: if you get into a bar fight, contain the situation and walk away if possible. If you must engage, you know what to do.*) They will give you timelines early on from the perspective of the medical community. My non-medical opinion: (see disclaimer in Introduction) - gains are possible WAY beyond that. Ask me. Ask Matt. And I've heard a ton of anecdotal evidence from Survivors who have observed improvements in their status *decades* after injury.

BOOM.

(that's what David says when emphasizing a point.)

I will close with this:

Do it for yourself.

I just told you that someone's watching you. Even if you don't have an eagle-eyed kid watching your every move, *someone* from your family/friend group will be watching how you handle your illness/injury, and how you decide to approach life afterwards. HOWEVER, the best reason to pursue Recovery is to *do it for YOURSELF.*

Of course your family will reap the benefits of your Recovery – logistically, higher mobility will likely make running a household easier in that fewer modifications need to be made to the house and to your routine. But there are workarounds for everything in case you never achieve that higher level of mobility. And the bottom line is NOT that you're hoping to not have to install permanent grab bars and ramps into your home – it's that if you don't even try to Recover, you will never know if more could have been possible.

Find out for *yourself.*

Ch. 4 How to Cultivate Survivor GRIT
MATT HANKEY

"Getting the trick is more important than falling on the concrete."

I was just getting to know Matt and was trying to learn about skateboarding. I had seen some videos of him skating prior to his AVM Rupture (April 6, 2012 – aka Shirley F. Wolf's Birthday – Shirley is the white wolf in all of my pics. Her middle name is FEROCIOUS), and I honestly did not know how a person learns how to skate. I was like, *Ummm….so Matt – I don't see any harnesses or anything. How do you train aerial awareness like that? Do you have a coach, etc.?*

He explained that the way you learn is pretty casual: you might watch some vids and then you watch your friends do it, and then you GO FOR IT.

Me: *Ummmm….there is no mat or a foam pit under the ramp. It looks rather dangerous.*

That's when he told me, "Getting the trick is more important than falling on the concrete."

This statement told me a couple things:

A. <u>Matt has a physical predisposition towards athleticism.</u>

I asked him some nosey questions in the beginning that only another Survivor can ask and I KNEW that <u>he remembered</u> what it felt like to be in the air, to have enough time to achieve a fantastic body line, and to casually reconnect with his spinning skateboard so he could touch down on the ramp or on the inside of the pool.

I would never classify myself as having been an athlete in my youth. I certainly would never appropriate the title of "gymnast." It was Trainer David (after 2 months of observing my post-AVM mobility) who told me he knew I had done gymnastics bc I retained some of the movement patterns. *See Vol. 2- Learning How to Live ch. 5. "Appraisal" and ch. 13 "Cartwheel."* I had only done gymnastics very briefly and very badly (not exaggerating), and had never gotten airborne in any meaningful way. However, I still remember how certain things feel and I use this knowledge daily – it's how I learned to walk in the first place (press your digits into the ground).

Physical memory is very powerful, but it's also quite torturous - I thought it would be especially difficult for Matt to recall what it feels like to take flight while remaining tethered to his chair.

B. <u>Matt has the Grit to go far.</u>

He told me that thing about getting the trick as if the concrete were a completely immaterial factor in the equation. He used an extremely matter of fact tone. I am a contingency planner and like to know the safety measures in place in every scenario. But sometimes you just gotta go ahead and do stuff.

This is the attitude Matt grew up with. Granted, he was 16 when he bled and had immense physical confidence (with good reason) – youth and natural ability are enviable advantages, but achieving a higher level of skill like he did takes GRIT.

You have to apply yourself and work hard to be good at anything in general. Yes, some people are naturally inclined enough to make things look effortless, but even the most gifted among us are improved by practice.

Matt's skater attitude indicated to me that he had already decided what was the "more important" thing, and if given the opportunity, he'd pursue it relentlessly.

I knew that my job was to *create* that opportunity.

Matt was 16 when he bled. When you're still in high school you have nothing – you're still a kid. You don't

have a career, you don't have your own insurance, etc.
I was an adult when I got sick – I had a profession,
savings, and a strong sense of self-identity and future
direction. Getting sick was....[there's no word in the
English language adequate to describe this.] But Matt
Hankey was the one who told me I wasn't alone. I
prayed about if and how I should help him, and
eventually we launched the Original Shredded Grace.
(See ch. 1. "Introduction – Welcome to the Club").

It was a success – we met our fundraising goal of $8k
and then had an extra $1k to kick off Shredded Grace
Phase 2: The Black Hole.   FYI, $8k is a drop in the
bucket – you really have to understand that this is a
black hole of need. My own medical needs change
daily, and the things I see improvement from are now
funded 100% personally.

I retain somewhat of an old-fashioned aversion to
discussing money matters – to me it feels somewhat
vulgar – but it's an extremely relevant topic in
Survivorship.

I am very grateful that I had the liberty to pursue my
Recovery full time bc although I am no longer
employable I had savings, MommyDaddy gave me a
home, and I had zero financial or social obligations at
the time of my injury. Now that I am no longer able to
do so, I understand that it is a privilege to be able to
earn a living. But I am limited by the fall-out from that
thing that exploded in my head, and so I've tried to

become a contributing member of society in other ways – ways that allow me to simply disappear when new health complications crop up or old ones make a fuss.

Another reason I'm grateful that I had savings is that it allowed me to self-fund *Learning How/Shredded Grace.* Let's speak frankly: I have specific beliefs about God and I like to talk about them. Ummmmm....I was going to be a *missionary*, after all. It's not like I can hide that fact. I tried for a while, actually – it didn't work out. And I like to be super up-front about it with all with my friends, especially when I ask them to let me write about them. I always like to give them a choice. The stuff I say is what *I believe* – I am not putting words in anyone else's mouth. And it has been important to me from the beginning to be extremely open about it and to make sure I paid for all of this stuff (the books, the online activities) myself.

When I first started writing I got an email from a woman in Israel demanding, *WHERE is your Paypal button?!?!? I want to donate!!!* It was the kindest thing. I informed her that I did not accept donations – however, all my books are on Amazon (Search: *Ann T. Ning Tan*) and are always non profit, but the proceeds don't go to me, they go to other causes – lately we are Helping Matt Walk Again!! And now we are helping build Discovery School in Burundi!! But I told her that I was very grateful to not have to ask for donations to fund my own Recovery. That was several years ago, however – if the situation changes I will let you know. But in the meantime, I DO have a Paypal Button! It's right next to the Magic Wand at ShreddedGrace.com – everything goes straight into Matt's AVM Recovery Fund, which is stewarded by his friend's dad, Mark.

When I met Mark (over email) he explained his role by saying, *My job is to make sure that this money get's spent on stuff that works.* I was THRILLED to hear this bc even *I* thought it was kind of weird for a complete stranger (Matt and I have never met) to approach this kid (I know he's technically not a kid anymore) and be all, *Hey – let's do a project!! Can you send me your financial information so I can set it up?!?!*

I had no idea that Mark existed until I realized that Matt had this extra layer of protection built into his Recovery. This is *huge*. Let me just say again that people always have a *choice*. And when people opt in to help you, it is something a Survivor should honor. And I honor Mark and Krissy for seeing a need and stepping up to the plate.

After I presented my credentials, or at least explained myself in a way that showed I had Matt's best interests at heart, I was further thrilled to understand that not only did Matt have *protection*, he had *accountability*. Our credibility level just went through the roof. I call it the "Black Hole" of need jokingly. You might *feel* like you're tossing money into a black hole, but you can absolutely give with confidence. The funds pass through Mark's hands before they fund any Rehab Activities. And you can watch Matt's progress by following him on Facebook and Instagram. Seriously – his progress is AMAZING, but it makes sense to me given his history of athleticism and his attitude towards physicality in general. But let me be really clear: It is **consistent access to care** that is making this possible – you are making this happen. Thank you for your support.

Side note: When I say you are making "this" possible, "this" is never enough for people like me and Matt. We want more gains yesterday. But when I step back and just look at his posts on social media, the progress is clear, and I'm thrilled to watch this unfold. Keep on going, Matt!!

The bottom line here is that Grittiness does not happen in a vacuum. You might have a predisposition for Grittiness, but Grit alone does not a Recovery make. You need help from the people around you.

HOWEVER, there are Behaviors of Successful Survivorship that you *can* control bc they are your individual responsibility.

1. **How badly do you want this?**
   This question has the potential to be insulting. We are not talking about just *any* kind of

achievement, here – we are not even talking about the kind of achievement celebrated by a televised awards show, a banquet in Sweden, or a medal ceremony – although those achievements are very high, indeed.

Let me put this in perspective: the first dream I had in the hospital was that I was able to make it from the hospital bed to the restroom by myself using a walker. That was all I wanted – to be able to powder my nose in private. I am an adult. Using the toilet is not a group activity.

If someone had asked me, *How badly do you want this?* Early on I would have rolled my eyes bc no one could "want this" more.

Seriously? *Unless you have wept tears of shame and rage bc you got stuck in a bad situation and can't help yourself bc of your disability, you don't get to ask that question.*

But since I *have* done that, I'm going to go ahead and ask it. And if you're still insulted, I hereby apologize and state that I understand that my experience is not yours.

Only YOU can answer the question, *How badly do you want this?* It's like the question, *Is it okay that you lived? I certainly cannot answer it for you –* but I can tell you what happened to me.

One of my techniques to indicate fear at PT was to stall shamelessly in the early stages of learning to walk. I'd say, *Are you sure?* Andy Frankenstein just said YES, with a Coach R tone of utter finality, and I still pressed, *REALLY SURE?* Again the answer was a definitive *Yes*, so I clutched both of his forearms and shuffled gingerly while sweating bullets.

I then asked him if he had a Magic Wand to make people walk without actually, you know – *walking.* (This is why there is a Magic Wand at ShreddedGrace.com)

Andy: No. And there's no pill for that, either.

Boooo. I just wanted to make sure there was only that one way before I committed myself.

I was treated by another PT one day and I renewed my stalling technique when he told me to put my arms around his shoulders (we looked like we were dancing) and practice shifting my weight. *Are you SURE?* I asked the terror rising in me with each second that passed.

I'm sure. Are YOU sure? He countered.

Touché, mon ami. Well-played, R7, well-played.
(They all had numbers in the beginning, including
interns and techs. Andy is 6. I gave up after I
passed 50+ around 2013-14.)

Well, I said out loud as I sat on the edge of a
Treatment Mat, *I DO wanna walk **really badly**.
So, yeah – I'm sure.*

He had made me say it out loud – I still felt the
fear but I had decided to do it anyway bc I REALLY
wanted this. You might have a goal, and there
might be a risk that you might get hurt – but to
use Matt's turn of phrase, you decide what's
"more important" and focus on that. Only you
can decide how much effort you will devote to
this.

2. <u>Eyes on the Prize</u>

No matter how much you think about your Old
Life, it's not going to come back. I heard from a
reputable source based on a wide population
sample that it generally takes you X years to
accept your New Normal.
Yeah....ummmmm....that was a while ago for me
and I'm still waiting. My heart aches when I
remember the beautiful things I used to own, and
the complete freedom I enjoyed in my Old Life.
But I understand that those things are gone
forever, and it does no one (least of all myself) *any*

good for me to dwell on the past.

Yes, it's okay and even healthy to remember my Old Life and recognize those feelings of sad regret as valid. Because what happened is sad. I like to maintain a positive outlook but I assure you that I am not deceiving myself into a unicorns-and-rainbows state of mind as some kind of coping mechanism. I feel the full weight of my loss DEEPLY. But I have looked it full in the face, made decisions about what I think about what happened, and intentionally try not to dwell on the past unhealthily. If I talk about it it's to make sure people know I understand how bad things were so I can build my own credibility.

When I met Matt he was busy building an online presence based on the past – pre-AVM photos of him skating, airborne, strong, and free. This was out of necessity. He HAD to do what he could with what he had. But I know better than anyone else that seeing old pictures of yourself is not an exercise bathed in the rosy glow of sentimentality. It hurts. Every image HURTS. But Matt did it bc he was looking towards the future and his peeps are the Skating Community he grew up in. So OF COURSE he had to go through all those pictures and footage.

But it's a means to an end. And the goal is very much in the future. I knew his story would not end with him having to sit there and think of days gone by, and I have been privileged to help move this process along. Are we always going to remember our Old Lives? Yes. I, for one, will never forget – it will always make me sad and I do not apologize for that. But I know that the best is yet to come.

3. <u>Do what you have to do</u>

On Matt's 21st birthday I recorded a video greeting (it was easier than typing) and told him that I had just found Diahanne (aka "the Pool NINJA") who was excessively skilled in Hydro Therapy and would train him in a zero-gravity environment (the pool) so he could learn to walk again.

But Matt – don't freak out, but D works in a Nursing Home. But it's really close to you – Google told me it's very near your house. So I'm going to ask you to go to a Nursing Home for pool therapy.

I was concerned that Matt, being young and cool, might be averse to hanging out in a Nursing Home. But I was wholly unprepared for what happened next.

Hey, I know that place – he wrote me casually – *I USED TO LIVE THERE!!*

When I read that I threw up on my computer

(figuratively) and hit myself in the head repeatedly (literally). WHY WHY WHY. I cannot BELIEVE I did this. If I had known Matt had lived there I would have *never* asked him to go back.

They discussed putting me in a nursing home before I woke up. Mommy had indicated that this would not be entertained as an option for me. To this day if I say the words "Nursing Home," Mommy's posture changes and she assumes a subtle "Ready Stance," looking for whom to engage so she can protect me.

Matt had been placed in a nursing home soon after his bleed and started waking up there. He didn't understand. We have NEVER spoken about it – I read it in a news article online when I met him. We actually do not talk about the details of the early onset of our illnesses. He probably wouldn't care – we're to busy discussing other things – but I avoid talking about the early days on purpose. It's too sad for me because I remember things I wish I could forget, and I know he does, too. The confusion of waking up and not understanding your surroundings is especially emotionally raw for me. And I TOTALLY just asked him to go back to that nursing home.

But I KNEW Diahanne was The One. So even though I was appalled at myself and apologized profusely, I persisted in asking him to go back there. And you know what? He went. In fact, he's there several times a week – and the residents are encouraged by his work ethic and cheeky smile.

Side Note: Transportation

One of the challenges of Treatment is that even if you are able to find and have the means to pay for Treatment, you still have to get there. Sometimes Matt takes the bus. One day his speech deficits resulted in a miscommunication with the driver and he had to scoot his power chair (at least it's a power chair) an additional 30 minutes to get to the pool. He told me this story without a trace of self-pity. Because that is what GRIT looks like – you get it done.

So that week I mentioned casually to Mommy, *Matt took the bus to Therapy*. Bc I had been lobbying for the right to explore transportation options for a while. I was like, *If Matt did it......*So Joycee and I went for my first Metro ride in 12 years. ROTFLOL!! But most of the time Mommy or Daddy drives me bc this is part of their care for me.

However, I am still lobbying for the right to explore transportation options bc it is a very common thing for disabled people to use either specially designed public transportation tools (e.g. Metro Access in the D.C. area), or private transport arrangements. E.g. you can find a Companion who will drive you on Care.com or through a medical companion care company. You can also research resources specific to your community – ask around.

Back to the matter at hand: sometimes you gotta just get it done. Before we hit on the idea of Pool

Therapy and found Diahanne, I had sent Matt to go try his local AlterG – the antigravity treadmill I use and LOVE. The thing about the AlterG is that it requires a higher level of mobility than a weight-bearing harness device like the ZeroG. If you're in a harness the practitioner can reach over and move your legs for you. The AlterG requires that you must be able to get into the "cockpit," and then your legs are surrounded by a bubble. Matt sent me an SOS email that day bc he had struggled but been ultimately unable to be assisted into the AlterG. It had been an embarrassing moment. Everybody in the clinic could see that Matt couldn't get into the machine.

Again, I was horrified that I had set him up for this. But then I rallied and took the opportunity to tell him, *Hey – Matt, sorry, I should've mentioned this earlier but I forgot: We're going to have to look silly for this. Recovery means that you go out there and you let the people in the clinic, on the street, in the restaurant, at the store look at you as you try stuff. You might fail, but eventually you will learn how, and you'll succeed. But there is a painful but necessary process of looking and feeling potentially silly. Very. Silly.*

To illustrate this point and as a gesture of good faith I set about learning about skateboarding. Ruthie (my brother Ernie's wife) took me to a Skate Shop near their house and I bought my first pair of Stance socks. Coach R, a skateboarder, had educated me on them. So now they are all I wear. I then bought a dozen skater shoes – Vans and Nike. Okay not a dozen. But maybe 10. And I bought so many sunglasses Mommy told me I had to stop. But I LOVE the sunglasses. That's why in almost all of my social media pics I'm wearing shades.

I also bought 2 skateboards that were being sold to benefit Matt at the time. They arrived and I was like, *Dude – these things don't even have WHEELS. What is up with that?!?!* Since my "home" skate shop is in another state, Coach R told me to go to the Vans store at the mall, go to the back desk and request "trucks 'n wheels" for my two decks. So Ann and June (and their two daughters) took me to the Vans store to get this taken care of.

Thus outfitted, I planted one skateboard at the clinic with Randy, and kept one at home for my own photo-ops. Randy proceeded to stuff the board inside the AlterG to prove that it can be done – i.e. you can skate inside the AlterG – however, this is not a recommended application. Randy, after all, is a professional. He got me to stand on it once, after a lot of coaxing and fussing (on my part) – I wore my checkerboard Vans and Mathew (my photographer friend from church) documented the whole thing.

My favorite picture, however, was a selfie I took on a sunny day – I had just gotten home from training and I was wearing knee-high Star Wars stance socks. I pulled them up as high as they would go so they looked exceedingly awkward with the capri boot cut pants I was wearing. But I enjoyed the effect immensely and smiled for the camera. I posted it with the caption,

> Hey, Matt – this is what COMMITMENT looks like – take some notes.

That pic also made it into the Shredded Grace Trailer – go watch it on Youtube. So, yeah – if you're going to Recover, you have to be willing to look silly. You will also have to learn how to tolerate both fear and pain.

One day my back squat lacked depth and I was really wobbly at the bottom (even though it was shallow). David was not pleased bc he knew I could do MUCH better and this is an important movement for many reasons that translate directly to my quality of life.

D: What's wrong?
Me: I'm scared.
D: [leans in confidentially] Stop being a sissy. GET IT DONE.

He knows when to push me. I respond well to antagonism. I'm like, Oh, YEAH, Sister Maria?!?! I'll show YOU who's a sissy. (note, we really are a very cordial pair, you just have to be able to read into the bickering.)

Another day I was in a lot of pain (primarily the left hip). The left hip pain was old news to me and I thought I hid it reasonably well. I didn't realize that Randy could tell what was going on from the way I sat, and even breathed. After I ran and we trained he said simply, *I like the fact that even though you weren't feelin' it today you came in anyway and got it DONE.*

LOL – these guys have VERY different personalities but we have realized so much success bc they are essentially cut from the same cloth. They expect a lot, and they give a lot. I knew very early on that to reap the benefits of their expertise – and I planned on using them to the full extent of their professional abilities – I would have to work hard even if I didn't feel like it all the time. It's true for gains in any type of recovery: you have to show up and get it done.

...

WOW - I woke up in the middle of the night and realized that my statement, *you're going to have to learn to tolerate both fear and pain,* could be interpreted poorly. It sounds kind of hardcore in a strident sort of way – I don't mean that you should be tough for the sake of being tough. Don't get me wrong – mental toughness is a Very Good Thing, but I have made sure that my people push me beyond my perceived limits of fear and pain only in appropriate ways.

Both David and Randy have specific ideas on the level of pain/fear they will allow me to work with, and if it crosses the threshold they have in their mind, they have a way of reading this in me and making me stop even if I'm busy pretending I'm fine.

I watched Randy rehab a lot of injured pros. I pep-talked the last one, *Whatever the man says to do, just do it. He has specific ideas on what he wants to see, and when he wants to see it. He wants you to be confident and is building you up physically to achieve success. If it's not safe, he won't ask you to do it. In fact, he won't allow it at all.*

One day David was leading me towards a new squat PR. I hesitated and just stood there with one arm resting on the bar. I turned to him and said, *I'm not being sassy – this is an honest question: Why should I believe that I can do this?*

David's answer was simple: *You can do this bc your Coach has chosen this weight for you very carefully.*

There are SO MANY lessons to be learned on multiple levels from David's statement but I will refrain for now. We are moving on to number four....

4. <u>Work Hard</u>

You really DO have to work hard, you know. Look at Matt's Instagram feed - @hopeforhankey. Seriously Matt, I'm tired just looking at those vids. And the voice you hear in the background is most

often Diahanne ~~yelling at,~~ coaching him. LOL –
she cracks me up. I'm thrilled that I'm not the only
one who gets "encouraged" enthusiastically.

For real, I remember what it was like to try and
make one of your limbs do something and it
would do NOTHING. Or, it would do the wrong
thing. You're busy trying to send the signal from
your brain down your arm or leg, but it isn't
getting through.

*Side note: I love how I use the past tense, "I
remember when..." like it is a distant memory.
Sadly, I still struggle with motor skill malfunctions –
e.g. I was minding my own beeswax and the
ketchup bottle attacked me last week. #truestory*

Matt is making great progress. The way he moves
today is VERY different from what he was like a
year ago. This did not happen by accident. It's a
combination of expert care and a boatload of
elbow grease. And all those vids are not at the
nursing home, fyi. He's doing a lot of work at his
house, too.

Yes, we all have a ton of appointments. I still feel
overloaded with homework sometimes. It was
worse in the beginning. I was discharged from
inpatient with an entire binder of home exercises
and the homework kept on being piled on from
there. But here's an insider tip: DO YOUR

HOMEWORK. To the best of your ability, do everything you can.

On my first day after getting out of the hospital I started wheeling my chair up and down a 50-foot hallway vigorously, just to keep my blood moving. Ten laps with zero foot involvement. Arms only. I used to practice walking on my hands and doing handstand pirouettes in that hallway. I shoved that memory aside and propelled my wheelchair harder. When I started exercising I devoted myself to cycling on my recumbent bike and using my left hand to do things. I then worked up to the elliptical machine. I literally started at 50 paces. I increased by 50 until I could do 1000. I built my credibility (my parents saw me applying myself and were willing to come with me as I explored non-hospital based exercise options away from home) and my personal confidence one step at a time.

5. <u>Congratulations – you're PROOF. Now you can Encourage others.</u>

I've done this for almost 7 years. Matt's been able to work out with Diahanne for under 2 years, but the transformation is happening before our very eyes. He's proven that he's willing to put in the work, and he's seeing results. He KNOWs that life beyond the bleed is presenting itself to him, and he has greater mental liberty with which to consider his future simply bc he's getting the chance to answer the question – what will my future mobility look like?

When I told Matt about my new/old Survivor Friend, Marlene, Matt immediately said, *We should encourage her.* See that, people? This is the duty and privilege of Survivorship. We didn't die. We learn how to live. We show others the way. We cheer them on.

The first people to encourage me were other patients in the hospital. I was so distressed visually at first I did not have the awareness to know that everyone was observing me. But they were – anyone who doesn't fit the general patient profile attracts attention, and I was set apart simply by virtue of my age. One of the ones I actually noticed was a nice guy with one leg who was on the NuStep next to mine at The Place (4th hospital, Outpatient, Shady Grove Adventist). He was hilarious. He was seriously on that NuStep for like an entire HOUR. I sat down on the neighboring bike in-between sessions bc Andy Frankenstein had decreed that the break between OT and PT should be spent in exercise, not sitting in the waiting room. (I had a break bc I was discharged from ST after declining to work on my volume anymore and asking if she could teach me ASL and/or French.) So I did my duty while this amputee chatted on his cell-phone and did the

NuStep at the same time. *I'm at the gym*, he said – *I'm SUCH a Gym Rat*. And after he hung up he caught my attention and gave me an enthusiastic thumbs up accompanied by a wide smile. *You're doing GREAT. Keep it up.*

Ch. 5 The Problem of Pain
MY FAVORITE PAIN RELIEF PRODUCTS

Mobility came at a price for me: PAIN

This might not be the case for you – but I'm just telling you now so

1. In case it happens to you, you won't freak out like I did
2. If it happens you will remember this:

IT IS WORTH IT

Many of my friends do not have the option of mobility. They live with permanent or degenerative conditions. I had the privilege of walking again. It was explained to me early on in the hospital (once they convinced me I *couldn't* walk – I considered all those failed attempts to be flukes) that it was a reasonable goal for me to walk again. I told myself, if you have an option, you should exercise it. So I did.

A couple months after Andy taught me to walk (September 21, 2011) I could no longer suppress the limp in my left leg. The left hip had been aching for a while, but I managed to hide it until that day – so I told Andy that I was limping, and it was fine – I was going to limp as much as I wanted. That's why I call him Andy "Frankenstein." I am Igor.

The limp degenerated into some crazy behavior in my ankle (it started doing weird things like twisting while I was trying to walk), and I was having trouble weight bearing. Sometimes my left leg would just fold up like a card table. By the time I got to Meg a year or two later I had a very pronounced lean to the right, like the Tower of Pisa – MOMMY and BOO BOO NEVER TOLD ME THIS – they claim to have been "happy that I was walking" so they didn't think it was worth mentioning. *Your brain simply doesn't trust your left leg anymore*, she explained simply.

This made perfect sense to me. I added it to my list of mental questions:
1. Will I see that person again?
2. Will I see that place again?
3. Will my left leg bear my weight?

Since I got sick the answer to those questions had been NO way too many times. But the one thing that I got really used to having around was pain.

It came from starting to use my body in new ways. The pain is often in the left hip, but circulates around the body. When I go to a new provider and there is a pain diagram in the intake paperwork I'm like, *Ummm…..what am I supposed to do? Yes, I'm in pain, but it's not relevant for this particular appointment.*

I don't think my pain is that bad all the time, however. I'm not trying to be tough, I'm just saying that I very rarely have to go lie down from it. I did realize, however, that pain should not be ignored. Earlier in my Recovery I told the Guys, if I say, *I need to lie down* – that means I should lie on the floor within the next 10 seconds – there is no time to go to a treatment table or get a chair. At that point if I felt faint due to lack of food (*cough cough, sorry, Smurfette*) or from movement (my vision still made up and down or back-and-forth movements problematic, I started to feel sensations in my body that were, simply stated, scary. I knew what had happened last time I felt like that, and although I had been assured that nothing like that would ever happen again, I did not want to find out how a new scenario would unfold.

A couple years of work (exercise and nutrition) has made me able to tolerate a MUCH higher level of training and I no longer feel that sensation. I used to say it felt like my body was "shutting down" like it when I collapsed at work the morning my brain bled, but my MHP asked me to choose another (less incendiary, less "loaded") phrase. So now I call it The Tuning Fork Feeling – bc it's like someone struck a tuning fork on my ribs and I can feel the reverberations in my chest. Okay, fine, I no longer feel that sensation....often. A year ago I was feeling it so often that I demanded an MRI and the full work up in general. Everything was fine.

I was also dealing with some significant pain bc I was recovering from the labral tears in my left hip. At one point every joint in both legs was compromised. Coach R was in charge of rehabbing me and I could tell from the look in his eye that he just wanted to pop the lump in my knee bc we had decided that it was a cyst and one of his go-to problem solving methods is HULK SMASH. ROTFLOL. The thing is I used to occasionally get a lump on my left knee. This time I had a big one on my right, too. Both ankles were sad, the hips were not good, and I was getting all sorts of hot spots in the lower legs he had to work out.

So for a while I experimented with forearm crutches bc I was REALLY trying to avoid putting weight on my legs. The only thing is that if you have unequal motor control in your arms, forearm crutches are not a good option for you. Yup, learned that the hard way.

The right arm was pretty okay, but the left arm would stab wildly at the floor with the crutch, and it was just not a helpful thing, even if it *was* entertaining for bystanders. So I ordered a new rollator – the 3 – wheel kind. The funny thing is that Andy Frankenstein TOTALLY goes to my regular gym. I met him one day while I was on a treatment table and David was working on my hip. I sat up and the guy on the next table said, *Ann – it's me, Andy. I barely recognized you. Remember me from PT?*

Of COURSE I remembered him. You don't forget the person who taught you to walk as an adult. I'm just saying.

Andy, you're FAMOUS! I had just done an internal staff event at the gym and told them all about Andy Frankenstein. Andy now worked at the clinic of the hospital where my ortho surgeon was.

Coach Randy was the one who had originally told me that my gait had changed, the pain I was experiencing was different than the pain of the previous 5 years, and I should be properly checked out. So we went across the hall to my ortho (3 cheers for coordinated care), and the doc, who didn't do this type of surgery, ordered an MRA (the one that Randy claimed would not hurt) and referred me to another ortho surgeon. Dr. W. educated me on how labral tears affect many people, but I am not "many people." My body responds differently to things. I knew I had simply been using my body too long in abnormal ways. (But the good news is that I can still use it!!) He leveled with me on pain vs. functionality and said, well, I want to see how you respond to therapy before we consider surgery.

So I put Randy in charge of rehab 2x a week, and neither one of the guys let me lift or carry anything for 6-9 months. But at the right time they started building me back up. After only 2-3 months, however, I already feeling so much better that surgery was taken off the table as an option. Andy Frankenstein showed me how to get my 3-wheel walker off/on a curb and fixed my brakes. Then Trainer M opined that, *I don't like that walker, Ann. It goes too fast.* (I had asked Mark and Randy to do something to it, so M had the opportunity to test drive it.)

Me: Ummmm, Mark, it's a *walker*. How fast can it really go?

And then Trainer S (at David's gym – but fascinatingly she used to work for Coach R) picked Charles up (yes, my walker is named Charles, like my Rice Baby), and literally ran away with it. She hid it in a corner. D helped me find it. D also informed me that day that using the walker had messed my deadlift up. It had de-trained certain muscles. He wasn't telling me to stop using the walker, he was just informing me that there were new wrinkles in the situation so he'd have to train me differently.

I ditched the walker anyway. My pain levels were improving, and a change in my nutrition (approved by my PCP and Neuro and overseen by Jessica Smurfette, RD) – keto – led to a dramatic decrease in inflammation to the point that I stopped taking one of my muscle relaxant meds (I had seen more spasticity since the labral tears), and I no longer needed a paddle walker in the morning to get out of bed.

And then, a few months later, SPEED BUMP. Excruciating pain in my right shoulder and arm, sometimes left shoulder – due to stress and inappropriate breathing technique (6 years of it). I was *so sad*. In retrospect, the first sign of structural change was that my left shoulder started dragging more while running. The AlterG adjusts to your height. I started at an 11. On the day I met Coach Randy, he changed me to a 9 bc he likes you to wear the bubble low on the hips so you can move your arms ("you know, *athletically*" ROTFLOL). I later lowered the chassis to 7 bc I had really started using my arms and the left one still hung lower and it dragged on the AlterG bubble when I ran (I ended up with a hole in my left elbow once and learned my lesson. I stayed at 7 for 2 years. But something shifted last summer and I had to move down to a 6. I think that was the first sign that my shoulders had been impacted after all these years of Bad Breathing.

It was the right shoulder that first had major pain, though. David made breathing exercises mandatory, and did a TON of manual therapy while I just cried and tried to wriggle away. My PCP did everything to make sure this was not a pulmonary or cardiac issue. I went to see Dr. Cheryl, the chiro. I went back to see NP5 and MPH.

WOW. It's been rough. But you know what? I got better. The fact that I'm able to sit here typing this book (even if I have to break super often) is a triumph.

For a while there I literally just stopped all of my activities, including all computer usage and piano playing. I made a concerted effort to try and watch TV. But then I realized that pressing the buttons on the remote hurt.

So I instituted Family Movie Night and made Daddy do it. *BAHAHAHAHA!!*

Anyway, I'm telling you this stuff about the labral tears, my breathing and my shoulders/arm bc I want you to understand that yes, Mobility, and life in general, came at a price for me. There are physical consequences to living in a body like this and being able to enjoy a higher quality of life in general. But I am HAPPY and WILLING to do so.

Many people don't get that choice. But I did. So you'd better believe I'm gonna be grateful for it.

Further, please note my response to pain. The first time I was in pain I was TERRIFIED (see *Vol. 3 Learning How to Run* – "Introduction: He Chose to Help Me"). But then I got the full work up and when they failed to find anything structurally wrong with me I sought medical clearance to try and exercise as much as my heart desired, and then I did. (After CMD brought me to a place where I *could* – see *Vol 2. Learning How to Live* – "Ch. 5 Expect More".)

You want to be responsible – you should be guided by your Medical Team to make sure you are doing what you can to help yourself and stay safe.

But by the time I got around to the hip, breathing, shoulders thing I was not as scared. Well, I was definitely troubled when every joint in both legs became problematic, but I just prayed about it and said, *Lord, the physical parameters I'm dealing with are immaterial to you – I know I will get better to the extent that You have planned for me, and I'm cool with that. Help me to trust the people you've given me.*

Because, yes, I still do have to pray for God's help to trust them. Yes, they've proven themselves over and over, but I'm a tough customer, ya know?

This time, David is in charge (see Ch. 7 "I'll Fly Away") of Operation Lift and I told him several weeks ago, *I'm actually really excited bc I know it can happen – you guys wouldn't let me do ANYTHING for such a long time last year, but then you built me up again and I was stronger than ever.* He agreed – and opined that the rebuilding phase will likely go even faster this time.

So now that I've been doing this for a while I know that these changes in my pain landscape and physical situation will continue to happen and I will continue to handle them with the help of Team Tanimal. (Side note: what a blessing to have people to ask for help when you're in trouble!)

I also know, well, technically, MHP informed me, that when I am in pain I get depressed. This might be obvious, but living with a high level of chronic pain can be so draining that it can affect your attitude towards life and the people around you. It's in everyone's best interest to keep your pain under control. Do not let it rule you. It was a revelation to me when I found out that there were things I could do to make the pain better. Learning how to run, for instance, was HUGE – the freedom of movement (bc I use an AlterG and you can't fall out), is phenomenal. My joints get to move and be happy, and my mind gets free reign. It's pretty fantastic. I also devote myself to the following:

1. **Mindfulness/Meditation + Breathing** – When my breathing could no longer be ignored I started doing serious research into Mindfulness/Meditation. Actually, I had started this practice 6 months before but had stopped out of frustration. (Side note: it took me a while to figure it out – I had to do my own research and watch all of those explanatory animations on Headspace and YouTube. So if you're struggling with it, give it a fair chance – stick with it for at least 2 weeks. Also, meditation is not recommended during periods of SEVERE depression. Mild to

moderate is ok.)

Mindfulness (often referred to as a form of meditation) is a bit of a buzzword, but the research on it is growing and the practice is increasingly used in contexts like the U.S. Military, high-level sports performance, and public education. I approach it like I approach everything – through the lens of my faith – and find it to be an amazingly helpful tool.

I also started the practice of mindfulness simultaneously with concerted breathing exercises I had been taught in PT (but never did – see Vol. 2 *Learning How to Live* ch. 12 "Come with Me"), and that Trainer David resurrected with great alacrity. At a 2015 PT eval, my very knowledgeable PT informed me that my breathing was messed up – she could tell just by looking at me for 5 minutes that my parasympathetic nervous system (sometimes called the Rest and Digest system) was never being engaged bc I was obviously busy being in Fight of Flight *all the time*. I had nothing to say for myself, and Trainer David, who was my wingman that day, just stood there, smugly triumphant, bc he had been saying the same thing forever. Two years later, however, pain drove me to action – I could no longer afford to not fix my breathing. I said to him, *I need this taken care of. I cannot live like this.* (I meant that the pain and the impact on my functionality – no typing, cooking, piano, etc. was not acceptable). So I let him use me as a teaching example – apparently everyone else can see that my ribcage is not moving adequately. And I breathed into that balloon faithfully, counted my breaths until I confused myself, and let David actually move my ribcage for me. [Slit-Eye Emoji].

It's been a few months and my shoulders are SO MUCH better. I'm still practicing my breathing and mindfulness, though – but now they have been integrated into my day-to-day routine, which is ideal. If you're just starting out, though, here's a quick breathing recommendation: I had been taught a breathing and visualization technique for pain management by my 4th NeuroPsych a really long time ago. I still use it often, not only for pain, but just to get me calmer and more focused. The breathing technique is very common and has been very effective for me – just Google "478 breathing." You inhale for 4 seconds, hold for 7, exhale for 8.

2. <u>Hydrotherapy</u> – this is a fancy word for sitting in the hot tub at the gym. I used to do Pool Therapy like Matt does with Diahanne – this was when I was in treatment at NRH (The 5th Hospital, The National Rehabilitation Hospital in Washington, D.C.) I'd do land therapy and

pool therapy twice a week. PLUS I was in Vision Therapy twice a week and did Acupuncture and Cupping with CMD 2-3x a week. I have no idea how we did all that. Thanks for driving me, MommyDaddy!! Now I don't have a pool therapist – I just sit there bc the hot HOT water and the jets make me feel better. They keep Therapy pools hotter than regular pools. But I think the spa at the gym is hotter. But it's good for me. When I got the labral tears, but before Coach R made me go get examined, I was in that tub EVERY night at 8.30 pm. Not even kidding. It was the only thing that made me feel better. (Side note: I remember when my hip tore – yes, it was ready to tear after 5 years, but I remember a very strange sensation one day when I went to the park with Ruthie and the kids. There was a very steep hill – it was a beautiful day, and I was DETERMINED to go to the park with my babies. Sadly, the hill was a little much for me – I didn't fall, but I remember a little twist and then I was holding on to a railing doing that dry heaving thing, hoping that Ruthie wouldn't notice. She noticed. But she played it cool bc that's what I like ☺.) These days, both MHP and Mommy have decreed that I need to help myself by soaking in that tub. It's a bit of a production to bring all of my stuff and navigate the pool and showers mobility-wise, but it helps.

3. <u>Massage/Manual Therapy:</u> You know what massage is. The Internet told me that "Manual Therapy" *is a physical treatment ... to treat musculoskeletal pain and disability; it most commonly includes kneading and manipulation of muscles, joint mobilization and joint manipulation.* I had never been exposed to Manual Therapy prior to David. My opinion now is that you SHOULD NOT let just anyone do manual therapy on you without first evaluating their credentials. I did not know David. But the Lord protected me and brought me to an exceedingly skilled manual therapist who found my particular musculoskeletal situation to be FASCINATING. The Lord's protection took physical form in Daddy who, when David said, *Come over here to the table,* Daddy said innocently, *Can I come, too?* And then Daddy pretended to read a huge book (a commentary on Isaiah he used for all of his covert ops early in my recovery) while watching David work. This had never happened to me before – the ability to walk in and say *XYZ hurts. Please fix it.* And then he did.

It was even more astounding when I found out that there were other people who could do this, too!!!! MIND. BLOWN.

After a few months of training, Randy developed a sensitivity to changes in my stance/breathing that indicated that I was in pain but didn't want him to see. One day during Stretchy Time (assisted stretching post-run) he just said, *Let's see if we can make you more comfortable.* And when I found out that he was actually good at this and that he understood that I would not go quietly if he ever tried to make me not run, I asked him outright to fix stuff.

Side note: David tried to make me stop running once.
Me: *I'M NOT STOPPING, YOU CAN'T MAKE ME!!!*

But the CRAZIEST of them all is Gen, my former massage therapist – an ortho surgeon doing volunteer work. I knew from day 1 that Gen
A) has superhuman strength
B) is the most hilarious person EVER
C) uses all her medical knowledge to heal your body and make your life better
For real, tho – she is amazing. She is Gen from the dedication page of this book. AKA Crouching Tiger Hidden Dragon. I worked with her in 2014 or 2015. Not very long – but I seriously credit her with allowing my body to run. She specializes in the lower extremities

and addressed every issue as I started using my legs differently and asking more of my body. Basically, she'd let me tell her what I *thought* was wrong and then after observing my gait as I walked down the hall she'd make a decision and get to work. Reaching this higher level of mobility translated directly into quality of life for me. Thank you, Gen. xoxoxo

The rest of y'all (Sister Maria and Hulky) don't get xoxo. You get the Emoji with Slit Eyes.

Quotes from Manual Therapy:

Randy:
I won't kill you. (Sure, R, that's what you said last time.)
Are those my fingerprints? (Yes, R – and yet I sense no remorse.)

David:
Stop making that face. NO ONE wants to see your pain face.
Ann, what happened to your big boy pants?

Dr. Gen:
Me: *AAAHHHHH!!! Mommy Mommy Mommy Mommy Mommy*
Gen: *[Creepy Face/Voice] Mommy can't help you now.*

Gen: [observes my gait appraisingly] *You've got just a little bit of subluxation in the right hip. Don't worry, I'll put that right back in for you.*

Me: *Ummm, the last time that happened it wasn't a quick fix – they propped my shoulder up on a pillow so it knit back in (I was still asleep in the hospital).*

Gen: *Oh, no, see, you're AWAKE now. And in my line of work we can't just sit there and wait for stuff to knit back in. We to get you back out there on the field!!!*

Note: it was excruciating and I screamed a lot, but it worked. I was not even aware that anything had come out of alignment – I thought it was SUPPOSED to hurt that much when I walked in. But after my hour I walked over to the store next door to buy some Pink Cadillacs for Coach Randy. (I do not give David gummies bc he gummy shamed me once.) But I just walked the 20 feet to the next door, and I marched straight back to the Massage Place. Gen was in treatment so I left a message at the desk: "THANK YOU. It feels SO MUCH BETTER."

The moral of my story is that yes, Manual Therapy hurts, but it WORKS. What a thrill it was when I realized that I had found something that was truly effective.

Actually, acupuncture totally works, too – please, do go read Vol. 2 Learning How to Live – ch. 5 "Expect More". As with everything, choose your practitioner wisely. I got NINJA CMD!!! But I eventually stopped when my PTSD got all crazy and I got super scared of the needles. I was actually less scared of the cupping even though there was a lot of open flame action going on, but it still got under my skin. I can't bear it when my Mom takes a cake out of the oven. But if you're up for it, please research TCM. It allowed me to start this journey.

There are a few more tools I'd like you to know about. Please go look at the corresponding picture gallery at shreddedgrace.com and/or kindly proceed to Youtube for more information (@shreddedgrace). Please note that I am not affiliated with these companies in any way – these are simply the products I have found to be helpful, and I hope they help you, too.

1. **Heating Pad:** I use a plush, machine-washable, moist-heat pad by Sunbeam. There are many brands you can choose from. Old school heating pads are a crunchy plastic kind of thing. The machine-washable technology is SUPERB and the plushness is comforting.
2. **The Orb:** High Density Deep Tissue Massage Ball; $20 on Amazon as of 1.18 – I have a pink one and a blue one. I keep it next to my pillow.
3. **The Grid:** TriggerPoint's brand of Foam Roller; $30-$65 depending on length on Amazon as of 1.18; you can get a foam roller that's super cheap, however, David

recommended this one to me bc of the texture and the overall composition – this one is hardy and will last. David would like it if I foam rolled more. But I do it when I'm in pain – it really helps.

4. **Theracane**: David suggested this to me for my shoulders. But I first saw a version of this called the **Back Buddy** bc Boo Boo is addicted to hers. Now I have multiple. I had so many that I rehomed a few to Coach Randy, Bob, and N<3. But the Theracane has specific knobs and handles for you to work with. $20-$30 on Amazon as of 1.18

5. **Fred, my Arm Buddy** – Sorry, I forget what this is called, but it says ROM on the side (Range of Motion). It's for massaging your arm. The tendons in my right forearm get twisted if I type or play the piano too much. Or use my FAVORITE hair implement that Dr. Gen made me throw away. SNIFF.

6. **Healax**: a heated percussive shoulder massage device by Ceragem – I bought this for Daddy before I got sick, but now I love it. I forget how much I paid – it was a little pricey, but I had tried it and loved it so much that I bought one for Daddy, and one for me to take to Oregon. It has been WONDERFUL with my latest bout of shoulder pain. Chez Boo Boo recently bought another brand on Amazon, and the whole family loves it – right now there's one on Amazon for $45 as of 1.18

7. **Shiatsu Pillow:** I use a Homedics brand I got on QVC. I forget how much I paid. But I got one to keep in Maryland, and one to keep at Chez Boo Boo. When I started running I used it a lot on my legs. This Christmas when my situation declined, my core got squishy, and I started having back spasms I rediscovered this thing. It's heated. I HEART it. If I had a task, e.g. I have to pack my suitcase by 8.30 am or whatever, I could schedule this in and then do my job.

Ch. 6. Best Foot Forward
HOW TO USE A MEDICAL RESUME TO GET THE BEST CARE

Excerpt from email to David and Randy – May 2014

To: Sister Maria and Randall
Date: 5.27.14
Re: I'm coming home! / The hole in my head

> *Random thing I forgot to tell you: I have a hole in my*
> *head. Well, not really a hole, but a soft spot like a*
> *baby. It's at the base of the head, behind my left ear,*
> *where they did not replace the skull. It's supposed to be*
> *fine - I only mention it bc the scar has been bothering*
> *me and the whole thing grosses me out. I do not expect*
> *to fall on your watch, but in the event that I do, I'm*
> *supposed to not fall on my head, k? Thanks, atnt.*

Man Alive, our correspondence cracks me up. It
didn't even occur to me that this was a funny message
until lately. At the time I was just preparing to resume
training with the Guys after a 3 month hiatus (I had
gone to Oregon) and I realized I had forgotten to
share this relevant piece of information.

LOL! Thanks, guys – y'all are real good sports.

"I have a hole in my head" is an example of Relevant
Information. When you go see a Provider you want to
give him/her the information (s)he needs to treat you.
Delivering this information efficiently and making your

purpose clear in the visit is an invitation: you are *inviting* the professional to give you the best care possible.

I assume you want the best care. I am also assuming that the professional in question wants to provide the best level of care. This may or may not be true, however. They may feel the pressure to see as many patients as possible during the hour, they may have home stress to deal with that makes them want to just get the job done and get out of the office – whatever. There's no way that you can anticipate all of the issues going on, nor is it your responsibility to do so. What you can and SHOULD do is create an opportunity for the professional to perform at the best of his/her ability so that your health goals are met. The provider may or may not provide you with his/her best – but if whatever care they provide is inadequate, then you find someone else.

Sorry, that was kind of mean. But it's true – you are at liberty to find the provider who is the right fit for you. I used to belong to a well-established healthcare organization. I found that although the level of care provided was adequate for almost everyone else, I was very happy in the beginning, and I LOVED that information sharing thing they had going on, my needs were specialized to the point that I became willing to pay more – a LOT more – to get the level of care I need. And I am VERY happy with that decision.

As I have transitioned to new medical teams a few times in my Recovery, I have come to rely on my Medical Resume as the best way to invite new providers to help me. It requires you to prepare for every appointment, which is a good thing. You must verbalize why you are there and write it down. I love it when they just read my question and answer out loud right then and there. Pre-work on my part actually makes the appointment itself very low-stress. I don't have to remember things, which is good, bc I already wrote it all down.

It also requires you to decide beforehand what information is relevant to the provider. I am totally fine with information sharing and encourage it – give me a waiver and I'll sign it. Please!! Send a consult note to my PCP. I'd love that! But not every doc needs to know everything, especially if your chart is HUGE. Let's go back to the Hole in the Head example.

I forgot to tell my new chiro, Dr. Cheryl, that I have a hole in my head. Oops. My bad. I remembered when I went to her for my shoulder and arm pain and whatever she was doing involved some almost touching of the head area. Now, they didn't put the skull back bc of the location of my AVM. Apparently the muscles are super strong there so they closed up just fine. They kept it open in the first place so they could scan me after surgery and if they saw anything left in there they'd go back in. Dr. Dogan got everything the first time, so there was no need to go in again, but there was also no need to replace the skull. Everything is fine and dandy. I never even had to wear the Brain Injury Helmet.

Side note : Matt wore the helmet for a while. He has a hole in his head, too, but they patched it up. I think it's some kind of Kevlar composite. *Oooh,* I told him – *that's very Batman.*

Anyway, even though the hole in my head is fine, it still grosses me out. Ugh. Yucky. The first time I touched it (by accident) I was SO grossed out. And if someone touches my head my instinct is to FIGHT. So it's only fair that practitioners who might come into contact with my skull should receive fair warning.

Well, I had never given Dr. Cheryl my Medical Resume. My bad. I was experimenting to see what happened if I *didn't* use it. Answer: my intake paperwork made me look like a COMPLETE FREAK SHOW and I forgot the relevant information to tell her to help her treat me. Bc of my medical history, intake paperwork that might be illuminating and very helpful for the majority of your patient population might end up looking confusing on me bc I read it wrong or got tired and circled Every Symptom or colored in the ENTIRE Pain Diagram. I do not intentionally misrepresent myself in intake paperwork, however, most intake paperwork does not provide an accurate picture of my health situation – which is why I should

101

consistently use my Medical Resume. Sorry, Dr. Cheryl! Good thing she's cool – I told her about the hole in my head while I was on the treatment table. And she was like, *Ummmmm....Oh, okay – you have a hole in your head? SMH. You're a mess.*

I had nothing to say for myself.

But the fact that I have a hole in my head is immaterial to other providers. Example: My Endocrinologist. He treats me for my purported HypoParathyroidism. I say "purported" bc if I have it, it's really mild. He's super nice and the first day I saw him I brought my Medical Resume and I really appreciated that he combed through it right then and there (it was only ¾ of a page), and made little notes. A year later I was in his office struggling with some symptoms. I had already gone through the information he needed, but now was the time to highlight another portion of the Medical Resume: The Goal Statement.

Essentially, this is the part where you say what you need.

So I said, *Dr. T – will you please do everything you can to assure me that symptoms XYZ are not related to anything from the Endocrinology perspective? My health situation is unusual, so please think out of the box.*

I know – I'm SO DEMANDING!! But I really wanted to get to the bottom of this, so I threw the gauntlet down. And Dr. T, being a high-level practitioner, rose to the challenge. He processed my request mentally and said out loud, *Well, we tested for A and B – these are the most obvious things. If we are thinking out of the box we should also test for C and D.*

Not everyone will be willing answer all of my questions, or to give me a thorough answer. But I plan to keep on asking. I am not saying everyone has to be a Rockstar, but I have developed a preference for very high skill levels. I know they exist in every area of medical specialty, and the depth of my need has driven me to seek them out.

If you are in a similar position, please consider using a Medical Resume. If you have a loved one facing a new health situation and (s)he is not able to do this, please be an Advocate.

504. How to Create and Use a Medical Resume

blog.annninglearninghow.com
Published November 30, 2016

I just got a text from my dear friend whose baby sister had brain surgery for a tumor several years ago and who is being advised by her medical team to get another surgery. It's an active tumor and symptoms (particularly eyesight) have been aggravated lately.

She was looking for someone to ask a second opinion so of course I was like, I LOVE my neuro. Go see her. And then I cried my eyes out. I still am. But then I figured I'd publish this post bc this method has been very helpful to me especially as I've met new docs and sought their advice concerning specific issues or procedures.

Update: No labral tear hip surgery for me, at least right now. Coach R's "Physical Therapy" is working. <u>He's an Athletic Trainer/medical professional</u> and all and knows what he's doing (it helps that he's got almost 3 years of data on my gait and is also a Strength Coach) but I maintain that he's totally just making this up in his head. Which is okay (I just like to say sassy things) since it's totally working. Sometimes I'm like, Owww! and he just looks at me with the slit eyes like, We should do this anyway. And one day my right leg FREAKED OUT so he just held the patella in place or something and made me finish the set.
If you're wondering how Trainer D and Smurfette are doing, they are fine and dandy. Except Animal Muppet yelled at me for a WHOLE HOUR a couple weeks ago bc he found out I

had stopped eating food again.

Quote from yesterday: How are your neurotransmitters?

Seriously, D – I am so embarrassed for you right now. Who asks that sort of thing? I don't even know what that means.

Meanwhile, I'm much more interested in the fact that Smurfette is rocking a new long bob after donating her curls to Locks of Love. High 5, Smurfette!!

...

Back to the Medical Resume thing: Mine has become much shorter over the years. Assume the doc will only glance at it briefly. What do you want them to know, and what do YOU want to know? Go in there with a goal (e.g. Information on Pros and Cons of X, Images and Tests, advice on how to approach a problem) and signal intent to pursue this seriously by managing your own time and the doctor's schedule by accomplishing your agenda and getting what you need with a minimum of fuss. If you lay it out on paper they know you mean business and can serve you better and faster. Also, bring a friend or family member so you can compare notes later.

This image is an example – it's what I used for my Ortho Surgeon. *Please go to shreddedgrace.com to see the Medical Resume.*

I know, I know – the majority of the population will not need a Medical Resume. But there are some of us who are so EXCRUCIATINGLY COOL that we will have a template we customize for each new doctor. This is a tool you can use to help yourself get the level of care you want. It's also a great idea for a family member of friend to do for a loved one who is not able to create one for him/herself, and also for people facing a new diagnosis. It keeps everyone on track at the appointment, especially if you're new at this and nervous, or an old hand…frankly, I'm ALWAYS nervous.

Ch. 7 I'll Fly Away
How Mental Health has Impacted my Recovery
P the Marine

P: *Hey - I found my nunchucks!! I was wondering where they were.*

I had just gotten an email from my apartment manager saying there was a flood situation in my home due to a frozen pipe that burst. My coworker, P, had said, *Let's go get a flashlight from my trunk – you should at least have that.* And as we stood in the dark parking lot she dug around in her car and triumphantly found two rods bound together by a chain.

Me: *Ummm....P? Why do have nunchucks?*

P: [matter-of-factly] *You know – for self-defense.*

Me: [watching with big eyes as she swung them casually to demonstrate] *Oh, okay.*

I have been very vocal that one of the joys of Recovery has been that God gave me friends post-AVM. Well, it was a surprising gift when P - a friend from my Old Life – stepped forward when I got sick and showed me the ropes after I got diagnosed with PTSD.

P is a Marine and served our country all over the world doing things I don't understand, but the end result is that she knows a lot of things – e.g. how to order street food in the local language in Asia (she's a gifted linguist), and how to use nunchucks. On the Veterans day before I got sick she was wearing a plain red shirt with her military ribbon bar. "Hey, P," I asked while we stood in the hall with our laptops under our arms and waited for a meeting to start, "What does that one mean?" I pointed to a corner.

She looked down to where I was pointing and said, "That one means that I saved a friend's life without getting killed myself."

Me: [Gulp].

To the men and women in our Armed Forces, *Thank you for your service.*

We hear this phrase often, but I hope you know I really REALLY mean it. Thank you.

P got PTSD while she traveled and did all those things as a Marine a few decades ago. At that time no one talked about PTSD. There were no resources to help Veterans who were coming home. She learned about what it means to live like this through experience and I will always be grateful that she shared her journey with me.

Sometimes I just had to retreat. I had to sit in my closet with a blanket over my head, and after a week or so I felt better, and I'd get up and go outside again.

When she emailed me this description it was like a light bulb went off in my head. *SHE CHOSE.* Yes, she needed to go inside a dark room and hide for a while, but at a certain point *she decided to get up, open the door and rejoin life.*

Once I was diagnosed with (Delayed Onset) PTSD and P explained her experience to me I realized that for the first time since my brain bled, I felt like I had a choice. My own sense of Agency hit me like a lightning bolt. I had sought professional help bc I seriously felt like I was going CRAZY. I was extremely jumpy, I *always* watched my back, and my emotions would take me for a ride.

But once I knew that this thing was called PTSD, I told myself, *it has been diagnosed, therefore it can be treated.* And I had P to explain it to me – what a gift. Her story about the closet and the blanket was so *real.* And it was only after she shared that with me that I decided to get up and fight.

I will back up and explain this better, but first I want to point out that P got PTSD in combat. I got PTSD bc of Medical Trauma. But it doesn't matter what you're struggling with, or why you have it – there are a billion reasons why you could struggle with mental health issues – some reasons are circumstantial, some are not. Let me go back to Ch. 1 – Introduction – Rule 5. DO NOT COMPARE. Reminder: We are not comparing how much we have suffered, the nature of our injuries, or the trajectory of our recoveries. What concerns you, concerns YOU. It is the cry of every human heart to have their concerns treated with dignity and respect. That's why I'm writing this chapter.

I struggle with MENTAL HEALTH ISSUES.

See? I said it out loud. And my main goal in writing about it is to say to anyone out there sitting in that closet with a blanket over his/her head – there are a TON of resources available to help you. Don't be afraid, and never EVER feel ashamed to ask for help.

There are a lot of reasons to feel ashamed – especially for someone with my personality type and from my faith background. But I became so desperate for help that it didn't matter. This is what happened.

- April 7, 2011 (Portland, OR)– AVM Rupture + Massive Stroke, Craniectomy
- I was asleep for over a month
- June 23, 2011 (Washington, DC area) – discharged from inpatient, Mommy Daddy

relocated me to their Empty Nest so they could take care of me

- April 1-7, 2014 (Portland, OR) – after 3 years of healing I returned to OR to dispose of my earthly possessions (the contents of my Apartment had been put into storage)
- Q3-Q4 2014 – I knew something was wrong. I couldn't settle down and do anything – I just felt very troubled
- Dec 2014 – started asking for help. Confided in close friends, asked Daddy to pray for me, consulted PCP and Neurologist
- Jan 2015 – formally diagnosed with Delayed Onset PTSD, began treatment
- 2016 – began Medication for PTSD Dreams and other symptoms
- Spring 2017 – PTSD symptoms came under control, I took a few months "vacation" from Treatment to try my wings
- Fall/Winter 2017-Present: Bumps in the road prompt me to get the full work-up physically and mentally returned to treatment with both MHP and NP5

This is what I learned.

1. <u>Healing happened before so I knew it could happen again</u>

This is probably not going to transfer to you, I'm just telling you what happened to me so you have the full context: In 2005-2006 I got myself into a situation where I was very v-e-r-y LOW. I'd say I was depressed (I'm not using that word in a clinical sense). I was working too much – it was my first job and I have always felt that there is something inherently virtuous about work. You should *work, work, work* as much as possible. But I failed to observe the simple rules God gave us to keep our bodies and minds healthy. I was young, eager to establish my work ethic, and thought that those rules did not apply to me.

I ended up paralyzed by the weight of my own expectations. I despaired of ever being happy or useful again. And I was SO ANNOYED at myself. Seriously? I still lived with my parents. No one was gonna starve. What in the world did I have to worry about?!?!

Well, despite all of my mean self-talk, God led me in a path that led to my healing. I did research on what a Christian is supposed to do when they feel so poorly. Basically, the scriptures assume that a believer should be able to handle a blade with some amount of deftness. I am talking, of course, about THE Blade, the Sword of the Spirit – the word of God. The scriptures are full of extremely martial language. I mean, just take the Psalms – the sweet Psalmist of Israel was David, the one who killed animals with his bare hands as a young shepherd, brought down Goliath with one stone,

111

ran for his life when Saul was chasing him, and was skilled in the art of war at all levels. His language is often steeped in the language of the foot-soldier, but as a King he commanded armies.

*Side note: I LOVE the verse, Your **gentleness** has made me great. Psalm 18.35. It's amazing that the combat is referenced metaphorically so often in the scriptures, but it is GENTLENESS that leads to greatness.*

I knew there was an element of warfare to the solution I was seeking in 2005-2006. So I set out to gain a baseline proficiency in wielding the Sword of the Spirit. Let's be real- though – I wasn't after any kind of finesse, I simply knew that the Word is inherently powerful – it's "living and powerful, sharper than any two-edged sword," it stands alone and does not require any human additions to "activate" it. And I was very afraid – of everything, but mostly of my own failure. And you might be able to ascertain right now that I am my own worst critic – I am SO MEAN to myself. So when I got scared I learned back then that this was not the time for a highly stylized fight scene where the antagonist strikes pretty poses and achieves a beautiful body line before dispatching the enemy. I memorized some of the simplest and most powerful verses in the Bible, ones I could legitimately claim as promises to a follower of Christ, and if I got into a tight spot I unsheathed the Sword and started hacking things up left and right.

Pretty? No. Effective? Yes.

There wasn't a whole lot of skill going on in this scenario. It was a very basic exercise. And it WORKED. God gave me a new song and a new life. And when my brain bled this is how I knew He could do it again.

2. Recognize when you're in Trouble.

I knew I was in trouble in Q3-Q4 2014. Granted, I started watching my back (literally twisting around in my chair to see who was behind me) as soon as I left the hospital. Before I knew how to walk I was easily startled, and because I was in a wheelchair the Fight or Flight response took the form of gripping my seat with both hands and rocking back and forth violently. Even now I will do that, even though I'm not in a wheelchair, I will just shiver and shake – old habits die hard. So it was not uncommon for me to exhibit signs of distress. However, as I prepared to go to Oregon these symptoms got worse.

Mommy Daddy had noticed that I wasn't just doing that rocking thing occasionally, it was happening more often. I was screaming loudly, too. I was very easily startled and frightened – and my feelings of helplessness due to my vision, hearing, and overall mobility deficits meant that I just communicated my horror in whatever ways I could. So Mommy decreed that after our 1-week Oregon trip (*See Vol. 3 – Learning How to Run: Life is My Sport – ch. 8 "The Full Workout"*) she and Daddy were sending me to Chez Boo Boo (my sister's house) for 2 months of R&R.

I enjoyed my time with my sister's family immensely. It began with a visit from ERKEP (my brother's family) and we had a huge celebration for Ed's birthday (Ed Blueberry, my horse/recovery buddy) – a.k.a. the anniversary of my AVM Rupture. Anniversaries like this are always hard, so from the beginning I named it "Ed's Birthday," and that year's them was *Despicable Me.* My sisters made hilarious minion cupcakes, etc. They went all out. Thank you!!

After I returned to MommyDaddy, though, the ensuing months did not make me feel better. I felt like there was an elephant sitting on my chest and I couldn't settle down to do anything. There was an oppressive cloud of fear-based gloom and doom that got in the way of all of the writing plans I had outlined in a special notebook I had bought after two weeks of crying at Chez Boo Boo. I had told myself, *Well, I got THAT (the Oregon Trip) out of the way. Now I get to do what I want!!* I had just met David and Randy and looked forward to seeing what they had in store for me. I had published my first book the year before and was mentally writing another.

I couldn't do any of it. Except train. Training became a Safe Place for me. It was instinct – I knew these guys were highly incentivized to not let anything happen to me during training. (This was before I even liked them, so I'm just talking about how they are obligated professionally to maintain a safe environment.) It helped that I asked them, for my own peace of mind, what procedures were in place should something acute happen.

Fascinatingly, Poor Randy responded with greater ease the first time I asked this question (Yes, I asked more than once). The first time was soon after we met in February or March, 2014. The second time I asked, more than three years later, he actually *knew* me so it was a painful thought. *Sorry, Coach R!* But I'm a contingency planner. After he shook off the dismay he switched gears, looked at me sideways and intoned, *Well....we ARE medical professionals.*

David, who works out of a Gym, not a medical clinic, gave me a step-by-step answer fresh from the EMT course he was finishing at school. So, yeah – I had come to depend on training as a safe environment where I didn't have to worry about my safety – *I have people for that* – and I would also learn physical skills that allowed me to navigate my world.

As a gesture of good faith – a signal that I was committed to working hard and getting better, and I intended to stick with them, at least for a while – I transitioned to the Full Disclosure Model in July 2014. I framed it in terms of goal-setting. *I need XYZ skills to live the life I want. You will understand why I want this life only in the context of my injury...* Etc. Etc. (*See Vol. 2 Learning How to Run: Life is My Sport – ch. 4 "Goal Setting."*) So I told them how I wanted to be a missionary and how God had put me in a wheelchair instead. I had purposefully avoided sharing this information with them bc A) it's rather a downer and B) I did not like either of them well enough to make the effort to tell them this.

Turns out that speaking openly with them was one of the smartest moves I've ever made. Everything got easier – I didn't need to remember who knew what, we just talked, and it was great. And I had the joy of watching them absorb this information, digest the magnitude of my situation, and renew their commitment to helping me heal. If anything, their resolution to see me Recover got even *stronger*.

But even though I felt supported in my health goals, something was still wrong. I had experienced my first flashback while with David – I was lying on a treatment table and as I stared at the ceiling I remembered the ceiling in The Valley. (I had brief moments of visual memory very early in the hospital even though I was mainly asleep). That was a bad moment. I didn't cry, but I paused long enough for D to know that something was happening.

"You don't have to explain," he said simply.

That's right, DAVID. I TOTALLY wrote that down.

After I transitioned to the Full Disclosure Model (FDM) with David and Randy in July 2014 my health took a HUGE hit. I mean, I had been feeling great – I had started running in earnest and my pain levels were very low. That's why I transitioned to the FDM in the first place – I figured I had to put all my cards on the table bc I was feeling great and wanted to ask them to help me use this opportunity up so I could reach my goals.

Speed bump!! I think it was related to the stress of all the emotional processing that accompanied the FDM (it was the first time I had verbalized many things about my injury) and also a bittersweet visit from my dear friends, the Johnsons (the missionary family in Burundi I had visited prior to my injury). The symptom flare up was excruciatingly painful and disappointing. I asked myself if it had been worth it.

One day in Dec 2014 during Stretchy Time (assisted stretching post-run) I observed to Coach Randy,

I'm pretty close to declaring the entirety of 2014 to be a wash-out...
I took some major hits this year...
(I was thinking specifically of the nose-dive I took after the FDM)
..But if I had another chance I'd do it all again IN A HEARTBEAT.

Side note: See Vol. 2 *Learning How to Run: Life is my Sport – Ch. 14 "In a Heartbeat."* The reason I wear a heartbeat (like on the cover of this book) is bc it matches the last chapter in Randy's book. That was the first thing I wrote in 2015 (when I wrote 3 volumes in rapid succession). I wrote that chapter while on vacation in FL, and I typed it up on my phone while I cried the whole time.

So even though I had decided within myself that I did not regret any decisions I had made, or the course of action I had pursued, I still felt AWFUL. But I would also like to be clear that if you HAVE done something wrong (a violation of your own conscience, or you have harmed another person with intent or by accident), there is a redemptive solution for this. But the point I'm making is not belief-specific. It's that in my own experience, the conviction that I had made the right choices did not absolve me of feeling like I was doing something wrong.

3. <u>Take the first step.</u>

The red flags glowed more glaringly scarlet as 2014 closed. We went to dinner (Mommy, Daddy, some siblings and grandkids.) I can't even remember which ones were there – I was so distressed I blocked most of it out. The only things I do remember are that I spent the entire meal

   a. One-Inch from Daddy's elbow – I was on his left and scooted my chair as close to his as possible, OR
   b. With my back against the wall – to give Daddy a break I scooted my chair up to the wall. Happily, we were in a private room so the walls were close – but we were in a *private* room at a favorite restaurant, i.e. this was not a case of feeling legitimately threatened by the presence of ominous strangers. I just NEEDED to have my back covered.

One Sunday night at church June looked at me and just said, *I'm sorry. I know you're tired.* And she gave me a hug.

SNIFF.

When I got sick in Oregon, June and J-P had flown out to Portland to support my parents. They sat with me at VIBRA (2nd hospital) while I was still asleep – and even though I have no visual memory of them I knew they were there (see ch. 13 – "What to do when SYL is Asleep in the Hospital").

June has known me since childhood. She could tell from the look in my eyes that something was wrong. I thanked her for the hug, and just for *knowing*. One thing I've learned from this, and that has been confirmed by Team Tanimal, is that I have a *phenomenal* friend group. We grew up together and love one another in a way we didn't know was extraordinary until we got a little older and other people started telling us that the way we support and help each other is something special and we should be grateful for it.

I explained to June, *I feel like when Noah sent the dove out of the ark after the flood to see if the waters had receded but the dove came back bc there was "no resting place for the sole of her foot," Genesis 8.9* – yes, I think in the KJV.

In addition to the Heartbeat I'm wearing a Dove on the cover of this book. I love the dove bc from the beginning of my Recovery I have thought of the verse,

Oh that I had wings like a dove! For then I would
fly away and be at rest.   Psalm 55.6

That wistfulness has never left me, nor do I expect
it to, even though I get stronger as the days pass.
Let's be real – Recovery is *a lot* of work. However,
the oppressiveness that threatened to crush me in
2014 has gotten lighter and lighter.

At the time, though, I was so distressed that I
consulted another couple of childhood friends
who both reasoned with me from scripture about
why I should be confident in my choices before
the Lord, and also encouraged me to seek
professional help since I was clearly unraveling.

And then I called in the Big Guns: Wily Coyote
himself, El Bandido – the man, the myth, the
LEGEND: Daddy. If you are unaware, my daddy is
super scary smart. He is the nicest man ever, but if
you approach a member of our family in a way he
does not like with what he deems to be intent to
harm, you had better just RUN AWAY QUICKLY bc
there is BLOOD IN THE WATER!!!But you'd never
know this bc Daddy flies beneath the radar, so
nobody sees him coming. When I got sick
Mommy cared for me by helping me brush my hair
and put on my pajamas in the hospital. Daddy's
form of care leaves a paper trail. (I found it once I
learned how to file. It was TERRIFYING.)

That said, my Daddy was deeply saddened when I got sick. Well, obviously, he's my dad. My *whole family* was…..it was very very sad. We Tans say "goodbye" to one another and blow kisses when we go to another part of the house. I did not know that this was not normal until I was in my late teens. But Daddy was *especially* sad.

That first year I gave him a hard time, but mostly unintentionally. He happened to drive me to some of my first anniversary doctor check ups. I just heard a lot of discouraging things at these appointments that I didn't want to hear. I'd hold it together but cry in the car. Daddy held my hand.

One day I was in the corner of the foyer (my designated exercise spot) where some of my Rehab tools had been positioned for easy access from my wheelchair. I was sitting there attempting to bounce a rainbow-colored ball. I was even using both hands, people – this should not have looked as pathetic as it did. Daddy came out of his room right at that second and saw me from the 2nd floor. He FLEW down the steps and I could tell from the look on his face he was troubled. But all he said was, "Sweetie, what are you doing?"

I said I was trying to bounce my ball and left it at that. And then Daddy disappeared. Mommy told me later that poor Daddy had been deeply grieved to see his daughter (whom he had raised to be a strong adult), trying desperately to bounce her ball while in her wheelchair. So he had gone upstairs to pray for me. After that incident I made a real effort to show more signs of life when Daddy was around. Basically, I like to sit next to him at his computer and tell him jokes.

But at the end of 2014 I decided that I was not in a position to hold back. So I went for it and said, *Daddy, I'm in trouble. I need you to pray for me.*

4. <u>You have Doctors for a reason.</u>

You can imagine that as soon as I said, "I'm in trouble," I had Daddy's full attention. Since the moment I got sick he has devoted himself to making sure I got the highest level of care in every context. I told him that I thought this was a Mental Health Issue, and I was going to start this process by talking to my PCP and Neurologist, and would he please pray for the Lord's guidance.

Daddy was ALL OVER THIS SITUATION. As was the rest of my family, although we had no experience in finding professional help prior to this. In light of this fact, if you are in a similar situation and don't know what to do – start with your doctors. They should point you in the right direction. I love my existing docs and when I am in the market for a new professional I begin by asking for a referral.

I made appointments with my PCP and my Neuro and they immediately grasped the situation. To them, of course it made sense that I would feel like this. I didn't tell them that in 2011, at my first outpatient hospital, my social worker had tried to get me to go to therapy or a support group.

I flatly refused [insert emoji with slit eyes] and said, *Getting ready to go anywhere is an Olympic Sport. Energy is like capital – there is a limited amount and I need to choose how to spend it wisely. I'm going to learn how to walk. Because there is one way out of this – to WALK, NOT to talk.*

Yeah, I know that was kind of mean. But I felt super strongly about it so I just said it. But I was incorrect. The way out of this situation was NOT just to walk. I learned how to walk and my problems did not magically disappear. But gaining more mobility satisfied some of my lower-level needs for independence, and after a 2-3 more years I was had the emotional bandwidth to *talk.*

Now if money is a problem, and/or you don't want to/can't talk to your doctor, research your options on your own. Or if you're being treated at a hospital, there was always a Social Worker assigned to me (both inpatient and outpatient) –

your LCSW would be a great place to start. There are digital therapy solutions if you are in a remote location or cannot leave your house. The point is, look it up. But in my own situation, I started with my referrals, Googled the list of options, compared credentials and areas of interest, prayed about which one to go with, and then jumped in.

5. <u>Know what you want.</u>

Because I am Bossy Smurf I had two things in mind when I approached my Intake appointment with my new MHP (Mental Health Professional)

A. I want her to opt-in to help me. So I spent a lot of time putting verbal opportunities in our conversation so she could say, *Your case is not fully aligned with my area of expertise, etc.* and then we could part ways with no awkwardness.

B. I was still extremely wary of MHPs in general bc I had no experience with Talk Therapy – I had seen 4 NeuroPsychs prior to this, but they had been very task-oriented relationships, e.g. cognitive evaluation, pain management, sleep hygiene, etc. No one had ever actually made me TALK about stuff [slit-eye emoji]. I was still unconvinced that talking about this situation would be a good thing. So when I went to my first appointment I said to myself – I want to learn specific skills/techniques to address my issues.

So this is what happened:
   A. She opted in. She signaled this during the first ten minutes by opening a copy of the DSM-V and reading me the definition of PTSD. I was not disagreeing that I had it – I just like to see/hear the source material whenever I can.
   B. She said, *if ABC happens you do XYZ.* When she gave me a piece of actionable information that I could use right away I was like, BINGO. I knew I was in the right place

6. Keep your Team informed.

So then we started a two-year process of really hardcore skill acquisition. You might well imagine that I'm rather a handful in Therapy. Any kind of therapy, but *especially* talk therapy/psychotherapy. But she stuck with me! And we began to see progress. *Side note: bc I am such a performance-oriented person I kept on feeling like I was "doing therapy wrong" – like I wasn't talking about things, or I was missing the point, etc. My MHP coached me through these feelings and the end result is that I really learned how to USE therapy – I'd go in, she'd give me some tools, and then I'd report back on what was helpful for me.*

However, things got worse before they got better, which makes total sense to me. This had happened when I did Vision Therapy – the structures in your brain that dictate how you use your eyes/the way you think, are intentionally being dismantled so that they can be rebuilt in new and healthy ways. It stands to reason that stuff is gonna shake loose during this process.

What this meant for me was that I started having flashbacks. I was also super nauseous as I dealt with all of this. So my MHP required me to inform David and Randy so they could make sure I was safe during training even though I was having more focus and balance problems. I tried to get out of it with Randy. I learned the hard way that when that man chooses to throw the gauntlet down he does so with unflinching enthusiasm. I was so shocked at how that situation played out I just email bombed David so I wouldn't have to talk to him in person. There were so many other, funnier, things to discuss when we did meet. (*See Vol. 2 Learning How to Live – "Introduction: Consider Yourself Informed".*)

Anyway, I'm glad my MHP made me tell David and Randy bc it was the smart/right thing to do. They need as much information as possible to do their jobs. When I have disclosed information to them they have expressed appreciation bc they really do need to know the details of my situation to write my exercise programs. I've come to view it as a standard professional courtesy. You need to tell everyone information that would be relevant to them (if in doubt, share it, or ask if they need to know – they don't want to be overloaded, but they will tell you what they need) to get the best care. From the medication standpoint you simply must share your drug list between doctors so you avoid any harmful interactions. But overall, the attitude I've encountered is that my people like to be informed of what's going on bc it helps to know the big picture as they take care of me.

7. <u>Be guided by the Professional(s)</u>

Things REALLY got interesting in July 2015 – I started having uber violent dreams. You do not need details on the dreams themselves. My Daddy asked me once and I refused to tell him. But I will just tell you about the first one:

It was like Goldilocks and the 3 Bears, except it was Goldilocks and The Bear MASSACRE, perpetrated by Baby Bear himself, who had an axe.

There was fluff. Fluff EVERYWHERE.

This was my first violent dream, and I didn't

consider it to be *that bad*, I mean c'mon – fluff everywhere? I thought it was kind of funny.

Ummmm... yeah. My medical team did not think it was funny. I walked in to see my Neuro that week and she was like, *You are REALLY popular – I've been getting phone calls about you all morning!!*

LOL. The short story is that my Healthcare Providers joined forces to MAKE me go to the psychiatrist and get some medication. My dream made one of them call the others saying, *I think Ann's in trouble. We need to help her.*

Neuro: *I told them (on the phone), I suggested going to see the psych to her a MONTH ago and I got SHOT DOWN.*
Me: I didn't shoot you down.
Neuro: Umm...*Ya kinda DID.*

Yeah, so I don't take very kindly to being told what to do. However, my point here is to PLEASE be guided by the professionals you have surrounded yourself with. They knew I was in trouble, and they knew the appropriate solution. When I asked Daddy for advice he said simply, *Well, if that's what they all recommend, then THAT'S WHAT WE'RE DOING!*

And so they directed me to the door of NP5 – he

probably wouldn't call himself a NeuroPsych, but I do. At first I fussed A LOT. I went on Medical Strike. It was not pretty. Ask Coach Randy. I hit him up to do my intake paperwork for me bc I REFUSED to explain this situation to anyone new. I was like, *I'm just gonna send NP5 a link to my collected works on Amazon and call it a day.* My MHP solved the problem by leaving him a long voicemail.

So I began drug therapy and continued my Talk Therapy. My MHP and NP5 did a great job educating me on how things were happening structurally in my brain that would be best addressed by a two-prong approach. There was a physical issue that required pharmaceutical intervention. I asked questions like, how do I know this medication is working? What do I look for, etc. and felt increasingly comfortable with the pharmaceutical route. P (my Marine friend and former colleague – the one with the nunchucks) had explained how medication had been crucial to her recovery.

It took about 18 months to 2 years during which I dreamed a lot, slept very little, and bought several pretty things on my phone in the middle of the night that I had sometimes had no recollection of when they arrived on my doorstep. At the beginning I actually bought crates of Sleepy Time Tea to give myself the illusion of a night-time ritual, but without having to actually *sleep*. I would sit at the table sipping my tea and tell Mommy, *I'm not going to bed. I don't want to see anymore.*

But I learned a lot – my MHP outfitted me with an entire toolkit to deal with all of the distressing PTSD-related things that happened during my day.

And for the night time hours, I worked out a system. It was actually Trainer D who told me about how to use a lucid dreaming technique. When my dreams were horrifically violent in a zero-sum game sort of way I decided that I would simply call on the Name of the Lord and wait to be rescued. (That technique TOTALLY worked for me in my dreams, FYI – the point is that you decide beforehand what you're gonna do, and then as the situation unfolds in your dream, you do it.) But for situations that were still very violent but could possibly be fought out of by human means I devised the Batphone system.

I bought a bunch of faux Blackberries from Amazon. They were red bc a Batphone *should* be red, and they were Blackberries bc that was the most affordable "display" option (these were the types of display phones they use in the store), and also bc I hate talking on the phone I'd be more likely to communicate via text, and I liked the feel of a physical keyboard. I proceeded to bedazzle the phones with rhinestone monograms and distributed them to my people – David, Randy, Smurfette, and Dr. Gen (aka Crouching Tiger Hidden Dragon). I informed them that if I were having an awful dream I'd call on them according to the services I required. FYI, this method totally worked, too. And even while dreaming I trained myself to take action – I summoned my people, and I even learned how to use my PTSD tools in my sleep.

Still, it was a harrowing time. For a while I was falling out of my bed bc I would jump out of my skin during a dream but was unable to catch my balance, so I fell out and ended up with bruises I couldn't hide. Coach Randy suggested to me once during Stretchy Time that maybe I should put the railings back on (when I got out of the hospital I had borrowed the railings from my little niece.)

Me: *[Turns face away with nose in the air.] We are no longer having this discussion.*

My MHP solved the problem my insisting that I put my bed up against the wall. Worked like a charm. Plus, my dreams started calming down on their own within the next 6 months.

8. <u>Enjoy your new freedom</u>

By the Spring of 2017 I knew something had changed for the better. I reflected on the 2+ years I had just spent in Therapy and viewed it as a success – it was a period of very hardcore skill acquisition. I'm not gonna lie – all that talking about my feelings and such was a *lot* harder than learning how to walk. And THAT'S saying something. So I lobbied for and received my discharge from MHP and NP5. I received a list of warning signs to look out for in case I needed help again.

I took the summer off and enjoyed my new freedom. The efforts of MHP and NP5 had allowed me to feel free to exercise the spiritual muscles I had taken such care in building prior to my illness. I felt like I had the room in my brain to think and the liberty in my heart to ponder everything that had happened and to refocus on the spiritual disciplines that had made me strong a decade before.

This process of rediscovery was thrilling – I had never thought it would be possible to *Reach Higher*. Addressing my mental health issues gave me the confidence in my Recovery to forge ahead. I approach everything from the framework of my beliefs and found that the techniques that I learned gained power from the perspective of my faith. And then I felt greater liberty in exercising my faith because I was in treatment. It was an empowering cycle.

However, I wanted some time to just concentrate on the habits of faith I had been unable to enjoy since the onset of my illness. And can I just say, I am SO GLAD I did that. I know it wouldn't have been possible apart from the new perspective I had gained from MHP and NP5. But by Fall/Winter 2017 I hit some circumstantial Speed Bumps I needed help with.

I followed the procedure and started with my PCP. I had gotten fully imaged less than a year before, but since I was having trouble breathing, etc. she explained that it behooved us to make sure nothing physical had changed. She also indicated that I should go see MHP and NP5. NP5 explained to me that if the symptoms had only persisted for a few days then he'd recommend continuing with the breathing and meditation exercises David was making me do, but symptoms that lasted several weeks like mine at least merited the consideration of pharmaceutical intervention.

I had to admit to myself that this problem had been documented for *years*. And it was David's moment of triumph bc in 2015 he had accompanied me to a PT Eval (See Vol. 2 Learning How to Live – ch. 12 "Come With Me"), during which my PT had informed me that my breathing was very seriously problematic. David had been telling me this all along. Poor Randy seemed to be extremely aware of respiratory patterns he didn't like (I started trying to breathe very softly around him a couple years ago). Let the record show that I have truly superior lung capacity. I can light up a spirometer like a CHRISTMAS TREE. I learned how to run for a *reason*, people. But sadly, that fantastic lung capacity was based on improper breathing technique – Stress Breathing that comes from being in Fight or Flight all the time. One week a long time ago both Mommy and David informed me, *You're breathing with your shoulders by your ears.*

I got away with it for years. 6, to be exact. But then the breathing thing manifested itself physically in the form of excruciating shoulder pain. My forearm started hurting and then my core got all squishy from lack of training, and I started having back spasms. It was AWFUL. But things are looking up!! I am back on meds and back in treatment – on a more sporadic schedule – with MHP. And I have made real progress with my breathing exercises, etc. and have started training again. This is my Instagram post from Jan 11, 2018.

"I can't live like this," I said to David yesterday. And then I remembered – I used to feel like this ALL THE TIME. 5 years ago I was in a ton of pain and could barely do anything. This recent episode was a brutal reminder of '12-'13. Then God directed my path to build my Recovery Infrastructure and I'm ready to declare that My Method WORKS. Team Tanimal is a well-oiled machine ROTFLOL. I have invited the highest levels of medical care into my situation and these people are **on point.** I don't tell you about everything, but this last speed bump was pretty bad – however, Operation Lift began yesterday. David is building me up again and I'm THRILLED.

And I'm not scared bc a year ago I truly thought I might lose it all but Randy rehabbed me until I was stronger than ever. So I know it can happen with the right help. David is in charge this time and says it's probably going to go faster (even though my core got floppy again and he's starting with super basic stuff). Soon I will launch Shredded Grace: Reaching Higher and explain "My Method" to encourage my Survivor friend, Marlene. David, Randy, and Matt are helping. "Operation Lift" doesn't just refer to #gains – it's a reference to the men who carried their paralytic friend's bed to where the Lord Jesus was speaking (Luke 5),lifted their friend onto the roof to bypass the crowd, removed some tiles, and lowered him down through the hole so he was right in front of the Lord, who said, "…Rise up and walk." I BEGGED God to give me an instant miracle when I woke up. But He chose to give me a miracle via ordinary means so I could participate, and I found out that His way is best. It's a big deal if you're in a #wheelchair when you get comfortable supporting your own body weight on your legs or using your arms. But it's even better when you get strong enough to lift another person. PS. Follow @shreddedgrace on Youtube, Facebook and Instagram. Even if you're not interested in Recovery, I promise to be WILDLY ENTERTAINING. This photo is a reject. I was voted down by my spirited "focus group" who said I have to look at the camera. Booo.
#avmsurvivor #strokesurvivor#lifeismysport #learninghowtoliv
e

Note: The Rejected Photo of me looking down is either on the back cover of this book or at shreddedgrace.com →media→photos

Ch. 8 The Power of Possibility
HOW TO UNLOCK THE POWER OF POSSIBILITY IN RECOVERY
A PRACTITIONER PEP TALK
COACH RANDY

Randy Rocha changed my life.

There. I said it.

I'm probably the only one who is reluctant to make a statement like this. Everyone else seems to have observed my progress over the past four years and come to this conclusion with zero hesitation. In fact, as I've rallied the troops to help me with this book I've been collecting comments from my Survivor friends who wish they had a Coach Randy, too.

Well, this is actually kind of hilarious bc I think I might have broken into a new market for Randy. His core patient population/clientele is elite athletes: ones who earn a living through their athleticism and/or represent their countries in international competition. He also grooms young hopefuls who want to play for their University and beyond. He is an Athletic Trainer who has served at increasingly prestigious levels of sport throughout his career, and then on the day we met he became a neurological specialist.

On that day he showed me around the clinic and I spent a few minutes on the elliptical machine. After he corrected my form (Trainer D had totally made the same adjustments 2 days prior), Randy leaned back, resting his arm on another machine and inquired casually,

R: What do you want to do that you can't do?

Me: *Everything.*

I should probably add that I was rolling my eyes internally. We never discussed this moment until I wrote this email almost 4 years later:

> *I did not understand the significance of your question until now. It was a big deal - I had NO IDEA Life could be different - I had a vague hope, but no notion of the logistics required to get there. And I'd NEVER dreamed of daring to ask a question like that. But you asked it, just standing there completely serious, like my answer actually mattered and it was information you'd work with. Man alive - as I'm typing this I'm getting upset again.*

> *I dismissed your question at the time bc I busy ignoring you, hoping you'd go away so I could just use the machine. I was not stupid enough to get my hopes up bc I'm mean like that and had been very disappointed during the course of the past 3 years. (They started telling me discouraging things after my 1st Anniversary. That was rather crushing.) I did NOT just fall off the turnip truck, and here comes Hulky talkin' 'bout, if you wanna do this*

RIGHT."

But I eventually came around....you know, after a few years.

*See Randy's book, Learning How Vol. 3: Learning How to Run – ch. 3 "If you want to do this right."

"If you want to do this RIGHT", is one of the most RIDICULOUS things Randy has ever said to me. And he has said some pretty out-there stuff, like the day he vowed to make an athlete out of me. It was July 2014, I had trained with him only 2 -3 months. We had met earlier that year and then I took a 3-month break to go to Oregon to dispose of my belongings (the things in my apartment when I got sick had been put into storage), and then visit Boo Boo (my sister). On my first day, Randy pushed the AlterG buttons for me because he intuited that I was to scared to do it myself. (Even though I had totally tried to get rid of him - no joke - he had insisted on staying.) He also made me let go of the chassis and encouraged me to, "move your arms – you know, *athletically.*" ROTFLOL – he cracks me up. Before I went to Portland I saw him once a week for just a month.

During my 3-month break I used an AlterG near Boo Boo's house at my vastly experienced Southern PT's clinic, although I wasn't actually receiving treatment. It was self-directed quality time with the AlterG and I was grateful for the quiet moments to think, and I forced myself to run in earnest.

On my first day back with Randy in June I could see a shadowy figure observing me intently as I ran. He liked what he saw. And then by July he knew that the parameters had revealed themselves to the point that he could make a decision. While I was on the leg press one day he informed me, "I'm going to make an athlete out of you."

I demurred and mumbled some kind of deflective and humorous response bc inside I was thinking, *Awww....that's sweet. What a nice, well-meaning sort of guy.*

Does that sound patronizing? I meant it to.

And then I got super mad. *SERIOUSLY?!?!? Who does this guy think he is?!?!?*

Does that sound mean? It was supposed to.

He's a man of *vision* – I'll give him that.

After the first anniversary of my injury I stopped believing anything anyone said to me about my physical condition bc I was tired of hearing what I didn't want to hear or getting my hopes up only to be disappointed. I had just made a lot of medical rounds for my 1-year check ups and heard a LOT of discouraging news. And I had also heard overly optimistic comments in the beginning that did not materialize for me.

Example: While I was an inpatient, someone explained, if you get just 1% better each day, after 100 days, you will be 100% better!

Maybe they didn't mean it literally, but I interpreted it literally. (Literalism is a hallmark of brain- injured behavior.) And I was grieved to find out that Recovery doesn't work that way. 1% better per day doesn't sound like a lot, right? But this model assumes the cumulative effect of a relentlessly upward trajectory. Everyone I've talked to has had a path more like mine – you gain 0.33% on Monday, and then its -7% on Tuesday. Up and down, back and forth. Sigh. It gets tiring.

So when Poor Randall vowed to make an athlete out of me I patronized him mentally, but when I was unable to sustain this more generous strain of thought I went *straight* for the jugular.

DON'T YOU DARE PROMISE ME ANYTHING, MISTER. No, Sir. Mamma didn't raise no fool. [insert emoji with the slit eyes]

And so I took my little notes on my phone and continued to write down *every* stupid thing he said. For the record, David said things that were even

MORE ridiculous. And I documented ALL OF THEM bc I was waiting for the day I got burned and then I would show them the list (it's actually an entire digital notebook) and say, *You lied to me. I don't like liars. Good thing I never liked you in the first place.*

Well, the athlete thing happened – see ch. 1 "What is your sport?" in Randy's book – and all sorts of other things happened, too. And I got tired of waiting to get burned so I found another use for all that documentation – Volumes 2 and 3.

And during this process both of these guys INSISTED on becoming my friends. I was not amused and fought hard. I had previously decided (in an unhealthy distortion of Survivor thinking) that all of this Recovery would be easier alone. I was tired of things/people disappearing from my life – this was exacerbated by the fact that I used to live on the west coast. As I settled in for the long haul of Recovery I planned my emotional safety by deciding that I would just use David and Randy for their professional skills.

Yeah, well, God had other plans.

But the ruthless evaluation process I subjected them to had its benefits. I walked away with a framework for understanding what makes a practitioner GREAT. I came to most of these conclusions as I observed Coach R over 3.5 years during which I built up from seeing him 1x/week to 3x/week. So, yeah – I've had a lot of opportunity to scrutinize him *mercilessly*. And when I really can't figure out why he made a certain decision etc. I just ask. It has all served to paint a fascinating portrait that can be learned from no matter what your profession.

Because I have been so blessed to work with David and Randy - two amazing practitioners who joined a long line of extremely proficient and hardcore PT's – I have decided that it's my duty to help raise up the next generation of practitioner. Not even kidding – I'm not being facetious here. I owe the health and fitness industries everything. And if you're interested in pursuing a career in this discipline, please continue reading for the behaviors you want to aim for.

But really, these concepts transfer very well to *any* discipline, and to life in general. After all, LIFE IS MY SPORT.

1. Build your Credibility

> *No one has any reason to believe anything you say unless they see the results for themselves.*

> Randy was explaining Athletic Trainer life to me. He started off serving local high schools, and then lesser-known private teams, MLS, and then he went to the Olympics with US Soccer. This progression was made possible by the fact that he built his credibility from the ground up.

A lot more was going on in the Training Room than the every day round of taping ankles, etc.

The best Professionals care for the whole athlete – Randy specializes in Strength & Conditioning, but he can also advise you (or the entire team) on nutrition, and you'd better fasten your seatbelt bc if you're not doing your very best he's gonna get inside your head and help you clear any mental roadblocks that are preventing you from reaching optimal performance.

Cough cough. Not that I know from experience. [Blinks]

Oh, yeah – and if you all suit up with the right technology and run around on the field, Randy will separate you into tiers of efficiency and then teach you how to maximize yours.

My advice: just do what the man says. Randy is a super swell guy, but is also a terrifying motivator. And he doesn't even use words – he has elevated non-verbal intimidation to an art form.

(Side Note: I recently found an old post on my Instagram account that says that in times of stress – when I'm not doing well physically – we revert to non verbal communication. We

basically just see who can stare the weaker one down during Stretchy Time. Unsusprisingly, I usually break first.)

ROTFLOL!! Man alive, Randy cracks me up. It's mostly unintentional, but whatever. He knows I'm not laughing *at* him.

No, wait – I kind of am.

But it's not malicious. I'm laughing bc we are such a HILARIOUSLY incongruent mobility match. Anyway, he started learning about all this in school just like everyone else in the beginning. (University of Maryland Kinesiology – Go Terps!) He was nerdily fascinated when he found out that the body actually works like the diagrams he studied in Anatomy class, and was able to apply that information to rehabilitate the bodies of injured athletes and build ones who were healthy but just wanted to be stronger and faster. Apparently he started making stuff up in his head like, if this muscle is doing ABC, then you defy it by doing XYZ. (He likes to use words like "defy" and "attack" e.g. "we will attack your deficits," "let me know if you want me to attack your body fat." – erm, as FUN as that sounds, no thanks, Randy – see ch. 10 – "Smurfette is trying to kill me")

He tried to explain his methodology to me once, but I wasn't following bc this is not my area of expertise. Or even general knowledge. It was like that time he tried to talk to me about my March Madness bracket. LOL. That was a short conversation.

So his mind works in a different way than most Athletic Trainers. I was thrilled that I don't need to understand it – I just show up and he takes care of the planning, the progression, etc. But when I say "he makes things up in his head," I mean it's an unexpected application of kinesiology concepts – he remains grounded in the community of knowledge that trained him to understand how the body works and how to safely get it to change. And then he'd tell people to do stuff, they'd see results, and he gradually kept on getting asked to do increasingly important things.

I was thrilled to find an Athletic Trainer when David got me kicked out of Rehab bc an AT is a medical professional and I felt safer in a clinic than in a regular gym. But still, Randy is a *Sports Medicine* guy – and I was deeply unimpressed by that. Me (internal, patronizing voice): *I'm sure you're a nice person and a reasonably proficient practitioner, but I need a neurological specialist. There is NOTHING you could say that could POSSIBLY interest me.*

I'm one tough customer. But Randy did the same thing he's done from the beginning – he built his credibility one day at a time.

2. Show me the Research

The research shows…

The first person to use this line on me was my beloved M37 – Meg Stevenson, my PT at NRH in 2012-13. It was right after my 1st year Anniversary and I was late to PT bc I had an appointment with my Rehab Doctor. I was very discouraged. That early on I was still polling on whether or not I would wear high heels again. I had an impressive collection of shoes before I got sick and in the early days I wondered if I'd ever wear my pretty slingbacks and chic pumps again. In the meantime I surfed Saks and Neiman Marcus online for flats.

I've since changed my mind – it's no longer important to me that I wear high heels again. I've tried a variety of flat shoes including "safer" profiles like driving mocs and boat shoes, but I gave up on experimentation in 2014. Even the sleek athleisure styles available now don't offer me the comfort and confidence I feel in a laced-up running or cross-training shoe. (And NO, David, I am NOT training barefoot.) I got more skittish when I had been walking long enough for my left ankle to need more stability, and especially when my left hip tore.

But back then I was still collecting opinions so I asked Meg, *Hey, Meggy – do you think I'm ever going to wear high heels again?*

There was a pensive pause, and then she said,

Well, the research shows [that given your ataxia your future body is likely going to struggle with this]…but if I were you I wouldn't give away all your shoes just yet.

Please pause: Everyone, I'd like you to go write down that phrase: THE RESEARCH SHOWS. When a patient asks you a hard question, you do not extrapolate based on your gut, even if your intentions are good and you want to encourage them – you fall back on the research. Cite "the research." Hide shamelessly behind the community of knowledge. Blame all those faceless, anonymous people for whatever comes out of your mouth next.

Because that's what I want to know – NOT what you hope will happen, but *what the research shows.* However, I appreciate how Meg left the door open for a miracle. We had worked together for a while and knew we spoke the same language – and the way she balanced clinical knowledge with personal encouragement really resonated with me.

Randy is the only other person to use this phrase on me. I had made some medical rounds in 2015 and had come away very sad from an appointment with a great physiatrist who was an accomplished athlete herself, but informed me that I was "pushing it" and should probably just sit down more.

If there's anything I abhor, it's being told to sit down. After I learned to walk my left hip went CRAZY and I was forced to sit down. I still cry over that. It was absolutely terrifying. But as I got the full work up, no doctor could find anything structurally wrong with me and the ortho doc cleared me to exercise as much as I wanted.

So I did.

The physiatrist who told me maybe I should sit down, also said that when I DID exercise, I should ice my hip every single time. I was horrified by this. For 4 years I had slept with a heating pad because heat was the only thing that helped me when I hurt at night, and now this doc was telling me that heat was the enemy.

I saw Coach R right after that appointment and informed him of the new protocol. Because he is a Nice Guy and Well-Mannered Gentleman, he accordingly brought out the ice after our session. But as he arranged the packs and set the timer he gently informed me, *You know, the latest research shows…..* [my summary: that ice might not be all it's cracked up to be in this context].

This taught me 2 things:

    A. Medical Professionals can have different opinions. It's the patient who must decide which advice to act on. Randy's superior knowledge of my gait decided the argument in his favor. Plus he hadn't been wrong yet (my documentation proved this) so I gave him the benefit of the doubt.

    B. Experienced and Well-Respected Practitioners keep abreast of developing research. I'm glad Randy reads this stuff, because I have zero interest in doing so. I like to say, "I have people for that," LOL.

My favorite part of that episode was that Randy just made a statement about the Research. He is not the type to get up in your grill and make value judgments. (Side note: *I'm the one who does that – Bossy Smurf LIVES!!*) Randy said his piece in his quietly helpful way and let me draw my own conclusions.

2 days later I informed him of my decision:

RANDY. I decided the Ice didn't help. And if anyone tries to take my heating pad away from me they're going to have to pry it out of my COLD DEAD FINGERS.

3. Make it Count

Don't submit too early.
Keep your guard up.
...
Make your opponent sorry (s)he messed with you.

I recently tried to give Randy a makeover to soften his image. I decided to do this while researching for his website (lifeismysport.org – this is the website I badgered him into letting me make) and realized that there were no useable images of him in cyberspace. They were scary and/or copyrighted. (Ok, there was only one tight-lipped US Soccer Mug Shot that really got on my nerves.) So I knew I had to take them myself or ask Mathew to do it. (Side note: I took Randy's book cover from the back on purpose. It's better for everyone that way. LOL)

He has a background in many sports, but he is first and foremost a wrestler. His decision-making process is largely informed by his participation in this sport while he was growing up. He also does weight certification for the wrestlers in our area, and coached his sons for a decade (Mrs. Coach R was the commissioner of the league. Not kidding).

He explained to me once that certain other sports just frustrate him – *because at least if you're losing a wrestling match you can still punish the other guy, even if he's technically going to win.*

Me: Ummmmm....okay. [blink blink]

But Coach R and I have only actually discussed a losing scenario that one time. Everything else he has explained to me concerns staying in the fight – e.g. *Don't submit too early, keep your guard up....*

And if you sense that something fishy is going on and your opponent has an unfair advantage that escaped the ref's eyes, *make the other guy sorry he came to your weight class.*

ROTFLOL!! Seriously – that man is SO FUNNY because when he says these things he's completely in earnest. And FYI his sons are like this, too. In Randy's house, soccer practice began early in childhood development because soon after a kid learns to walk, he's going to want to run and kick a ball. Randy's rule was that there was no left or right-footedness in his yard. You had to be able to score a goal with equal proficiency using either leg. Period. End of Story.

Side note: Randy's rule paid off. Just sayin'.

But back to the issue at hand. All this is informed by your ability to gauge the situation. Or if you're facing an issue at work you want to size the problem accurately so you can respond appropriately – be effective without overreacting.

Like Randy says, you gotta keep your guard up. Be aware. There is a constant process of re-evaluation going on because the situation is going to change – be it a wrestling match or a patient's case (like mine). This is where you get to show people that you can think on your feet. My Marketing Ninja professor told us to channel Wayne Gretzky and skate where the puck is going. Sorry I'm mixing my sports metaphors. I know – this is a mess. But the point I'm making is that people who have a keen ability to assess and reassess situations, anticipate what's going to happen next, and adjust their behavior accordingly achieve the best outcomes.

My situation has changed countless times since I met Randy. I told him I had been diagnosed with PTSD. I stopped eating food. I started having trouble breathing. I was totally nauseous and was dry heaving constantly. I got a couple of labral tears in my left hip.

What did Randy do? He carried my cough drops in his pocket, fetched me my ginger water, made sure I was not having any TIA episodes, and adjusted my workout program every time I needed an accommodation. The end result? I have seen a lot of ups and downs, but after 3.5 years of training I believe in the resilience of both body and mind because Randy walked me through this process, took all of the changes in stride, and never lost sight of the goal. Now people look at me and literally ask, "How did this happen?"

He has informed me of certain symptoms before I noticed them myself – e.g. when I got those tears in my hip. When he said I might be torn I was like, *Ummm....I've lived like this for a long time, and you're telling me this is DIFFERENT?* I humored him by going to the Ortho across the hall. He accompanied me for moral support, which was great, even though he totally perjured himself shamelessly when he said the MRA wouldn't hurt. FYI, Dr. Gen also said it wouldn't hurt, and then admitted she had told me a bold-faced falsehood so I wouldn't be scared. [insert emoji with slit eyes]

And after I got all the images done it turns out that R was right. I HATE IT when Randy is right.

I admitted (grudgingly) that he was correct again when he kicked me off the AlterG in April/May 2017 because I was running too much and he didn't like all the shin splints, adhesions, etc. As soon as he instituted the new rules I felt better. Notably, he did not limit the distance, only the duration – which was RandyCode for chop chop. Run faster. I told you he was a terrifying motivator. It's mostly bc he carries an appallingly heavy weight of expectation with him. That's why words aren't necessary – he gives off an air that less than 100% effort isn't an option you want to explore.

155

To be clear, I am NOT saying that every practitioner needs to be able to diagnose things without the aid of medical imaging technology. What I AM saying is that if you make a diagnosis or recommendation, base it on your careful observation of the situation taking into account all of the changes, and above all else – *mean what you say. If you tell a patient something, be prepared to stand behind it.*

In this line of work your decisions impact someone's body – in my case, my entire life. That's a heavy responsibility. I tried to communicate early on to Randy that the stakes were really high for me and I didn't have time for any shenanigans. He got the message and signaled back to me that he understood and would make every day count.

4. Raise the bar

That was INCREDIBLE.

[a month later]...

You can go faster.

It was the first time Randy asked me to do that thing where you stand by a line on the floor and jump over it, side-to-side, quickly. Except I did it very s-l-o-w-l-y while holding his hand. But the fact that I could do anything resembling that movement at all impressed him deeply.

Or so I thought.

Within one month Randy had settled within himself that what he had previously regarded with wide-eyed wonder was Old News. I noticed the verbal pattern and thought to myself, *Ummm…I kind of wish we could have spent some more time in the "incredible" phase. But I don't think that's how Coach R works.*

On my blog I wrote, "the tiger is showing his stripes." ROTFLOL!! The time for niceties was passed. Randy saw that he had more and more material to work with and he raised the bar accordingly. Still, he did so as only the King of Understatement can. He'd be holding my hand during ladder time, or kneeling next to me during Russian twists and say in that quiet, wistful voice, "You can go faster."

Bahahahaha!! Seriously, I think it's all in the delivery. I'm not making this up – it really *is* quiet and wistful. ROTFLOL.

In the winter of 2016 Randy was rehabbing me from a couple of labral tears in my left hip. One day we were walking over to the AlterG and he glanced over to me on his left and just said, *NO SPRINTING.*

To be clear, I can run only because a machine lets me. I heart the AlterG. And when I got injured I started running really light (at a much lower body weight %) but I still liked to run fast if I could get the left side under control. The tears resulted from usage, NOT overusage. As Trainer David put it, *It's clear that we are not going to train the abnormal joint movements out of you.* I use my joints in ways that most human beings do not. It caught up with me – my hip tore. FYI, running actually made it feel better. It's the regular stuff of life – walking, etc. – that tore it in the first place.

Anyway, Randy outlawed sprinting and some other stuff, and when I fussed he explained that sprinting was not necessary for me at that point since there is no good reason why I should ever have to run from the cops. He was going to build me up in a reasonable manner. And while I was visiting Boo Boo for 2 months I used the AlterG and rehabbed with my Southern PT.

I made great progress, and since Randy wasn't there to make me stop I ran fast. (But don't worry – I built it up in increments.) The first time I did it I emailed him like, "I sprinted today, and I'M NOT EVEN SORRY, neither...J/K. if you have any concerns, let me know, otherwise I'm gonna keep doing it."

Randy told me to be careful, etc. which I was, and then on the day I returned to the clinic he spent several minutes standing behind the AlterG and observing my feet through the bubble. I was sprinting. Or as close to sprinting as I'm ever going to get. I was going at my maximum speed. And all he said to me when he walked over to stand beside me was, "Your left foot is still winging out."

[blinks] Hey, Randy – I'm disabled....Did you forget?

(That's a real quote, BTW. I was just checking to make sure we were operating from the same information.)

I was too scared to get off the ground when I met him. Now I was running super fast and he was expecting higher and higher levels of performance. But that's EXACTLY what makes him different.

159

2 years after my injury I had sensed an attitude that I had received "enough" care –I had received more than my fair share of Recovery and conventional healthcare was not designed to expect more or pay for it. So I transitioned to a self-funded model (thank God I had savings from before I got sick) and never looked back.

It was like Randy had promised himself that he was going to see me get better. He probably did, actually. Well, he promised me outright, and as we have discussed, I responded internally with, *Don't you DARE promise me ANYTHING, mister.*

I honestly did not believe Randy's well-intentioned hopes would materialize. For a long time I was just training to see what would happen next. I knew he was constantly raising the bar – so Rehab/Training, although I was doing it all the time, was never boring. And if you've been in RecoveryLand for a while, you know that not being boring is high praise. But Randy wasn't just keeping things interesting – he kept raising the bar with the expectation that he'd train me to reach higher and higher levels of physicality. This mindset allows me to enjoy a quality of life no one expected for me.

5. Take risks

Day 1
Me: Your job is to help me not get too excited about things bc I kind of like to have my own way.
Randy: I'm all for the aggressive trying of things.....

Randy is a party waiting to happen. He's all about the "aggressive trying of things" and making your body function at a level you didn't think was possible. It was his idea for me to run on the AlterG and then train with him. Apparently he likes to extract performance from a fatigued system.

But as I observed him train all sorts of high-level athletes I concluded that Randy has specific ideas on what he wants to see, and WHEN he wants to see it. He wants to build your confidence, but at the right time – he wants you to take risks, but builds you up so that your body is strong enough to achieve success. And if you're not at that level he has fixed in his head as the definition of "safe," he will not allow you to do XYZ. But when he thinks you're ready, I repeat: just do what the man says – even if you're scared. He has chosen your level of risk (how far he will ask you to challenge yourself) very carefully.

161

I've never seen him be overtly crazy, but I know it's possible bc I prefer the brand of crazy that is a mark of my favorite kind of practitioner, and I tested him on day 1 to see if he fit the bill. I offered him a verbal fishing hook and he totally bit. So I knew what I was dealing with. But Randy knew instinctively that I would not respond well to sudden movements, so he has always maintained a very measured and deliberate bedside manner with me. Plus I told him that he was going to have to be the Adult in this situation on Day 1, so he knew that if anything he'd have to reel me in.

But here's the thing: He didn't know how this was going to turn out. He just saw that I needed help. And when I asked him if he'd train me, he said YES.

Randy was not trained in Neurological Rehabilitation. But he has become an expert in making bodies and minds stronger. So he knew that at some level, he could add value to my Recovery. He took a risk, and said yes.

I will be congratulating myself on the fact that he said yes, forever. Because he didn't HAVE to say yes. I set him up superbly with a verbal parachute that would allow him to say No if he wanted to. I like people to opt-in definitively.

But on that first day I could see the wheels in his mind turning madly as he stood in front of the elliptical, asking me what I wanted to be able to do, but couldn't yet. And then he proceeded to give me a full evaluation even though I had just come in to look at the AlterG.

He was calculating. Sometimes you have to take a risk to push forward in Recovery. However, be careful whom you trust, because that risk should be a calculated one. I had no idea that my life could be different from the way it was. But it took someone with a completely different perspective, the expertise to program me step-by-step, and the guts to take a risk in the first place, to unlock the power of possibility in my Recovery.

Ch. 9 How to Find Help
WHAT TO LOOK FOR WHEN YOU'RE RECRUITING TRAINER DAVID

Help me.....Help me...*H E L P M E !!!*

As soon as I woke up, this was the first thing I said. I just screamed it.

Or at least, I *thought* I did. Mommy recently told me that she never heard me say this. I guess it was all internal, then, because I remember very distinctly that I would see the figures of nurses walk around my bed and my silent pleas for help (I think I just wanted someone to snap their fingers and let me go back to my Old Life) went unanswered.

The very first time I was able to ask for help audibly, however, was at VIBRA (2nd Hospital). My Nurse Practitioner, J, was making his rounds – I recognized him visually even though I was just starting to wake up and as I passed within a foot of the head of my bed I whispered,

What do I do?

J had never heard my voice before, so he was not sure he had heard me correctly.

What do you do? He repeated.

164

I must have nodded or blinked or something. And when the magnitude of my question hit him he pulled a chair up next to my bed and sat down, rumpling his hair in a gesture I had already come to recognize as extremely characteristic. After a brief pause he explained,

Well, it's like you had a terrible fire in your house. The whole place is gutted – everything is just covered in water and there's still tons of smoke. Now that you're here, the extent to which you can lift the water and clear the smoke will determine how much you're going to recover.

Isn't that an interesting analogy? I was *just* regaining consciousness and had asked an extremely relevant question. It was simple, confiding, very childlike, and emotionally raw. He knew that I had asked bc I was scared. And he answered kindly, in a way that allowed me to understand the situation via pictures I painted in my mind, and invited me to bring the element of intentionality to my Recovery now that I was waking up.

The extent to which you can lift the water and clear the smoke.....

So from the beginning, (OHSU, the first hospital doesn't count bc I was truly asleep then), I inquired and was informed that there was a task at hand. And

I've carried that idea of intentionality in Recovery with me for 7 years.

David and I had a joint event this past summer. I got a text from him saying, *Hey, can you come to a lunch on July 25? We're supposed to talk about the Care Factor in Recovery.*

SURE!! I'd love to, I said – bc hanging out with Trainer D in any context is always fun – it doesn't really matter what the agenda is.

Still, I like to know the details and expectations regarding these events since this is what I do full-time (Write and speak about Survivorship and Recovery). And I am BOSSY SMURF.

He said, *there will be 4 or 5 people there.* They were interested in that vid we did for The Gym. (They had done a video segment on us a few months before. The Media People came out from Corporate and were so nice to us. Thank you, Heidi and Dave!!)

4-5 people, David said.

We walked into the room that summer day and there were 70.

SEVENTY. Not kidding.

He had also told me that we were should dress patriotically. Costumes were encouraged but not required. I was like, *You had BETTER be serious. Bc otherwise it's totally gonna be like Legally Blonde when Elle goes to the costume party that is not a costume party.*

He was serious. He wore a bald eagle Harley shirt and I tied a stars-and-stripes ribbon to my Hope for Hankey Tag and pinned it to my all-black uniform. When he showed up in red-white-and-blue I felt more comfortable. But when we entered the room – a beautiful exercise studio full of natural light that they also used for events – and I saw the crowd I immediately elbowed David and hissed, *You said there were only going to be 4-5 people!!!*

D: *What? I never said that.*

ROTFLOL.

Me [internal]: Rolls eyes.

Unsurprisingly, I had a paper trail (text string) that proved my point. But I let it drop – in the grand scheme of things it was unimportant and I actually thought it was pretty funny This is what hanging out with D is like – you never know what's going to happen next. The guys had trained me to the point that I was more physically confident in a crowd, and I was not feeling the oppression of PTSD since I was glued to Trainer D's elbow the whole time and there were many familiar faces in the audience.

We had been invited to a corporate quarterly with the heads of all the departments at every Gym in the mid-Atlantic region. It was SO nice of them to invite me. I was like, these kinds of quarterly events are what I'm used to from my Old Life but I would NEVER have invited a stranger to one. I guess David had vouched for me so we joined the troop of attendees. It was so nice and low key and not stressful at all. I ran my mouth for a bit. They gave David a special award. I cried and took pictures to send to Jessica bc I was so proud. And then they told everyone, *We're buying a copy of David's book for everyone in the room.*

Thank you! I was thrilled – my writing is always non profit, and their generous gift would Help Matt Walk Again.

During Q and A they asked David specifically, *What were you thinking when you met Ann?*

D: *Well....it was kind of like she was talking AT me with a list of requirements. And her manner implied that if I could not help her she'd find someone else.*

ROTFLOL!! David and I have actually never discussed the day we met. You can read about it in his book, Vol. 2 – *Learning How to Live*, ch. 2 *"Are You Ready?"* Hilariously, I had gone into that meeting determined to find help, and it was the first of what I assumed would be a long line of Gym/Personal Trainer Interviews. I signaled really hard to the market that I was ready to be taken to the next level of health. Inside, though, I was just hoping they wouldn't tell me to go home and sit down bc I was not a liability they were equipped to take on.

Erm…so my desperately hardcore stance was interpreted as more belligerent than I meant it to be.

But honestly, that's why I think David chose to train me. He could tell I had spirit. That yeah, I got sick, have a hole in my neck, and my balance is appalling, but I have some bite to me. Poor Coach Randy referred to it in the beginning euphemistically as *Personality.*

I consider it one of my highest privileges that I get to brighten these Guys' days in RecoveryLand. I'm actually quite adept at spreading cheer. *I DARE you to say anything different, D and R.* PS. It's a two way street – they totally brighten mine. ☺

David and I were invited to that event after I trained with him for almost four years. The Gym has watched our progress with interest. After a few months other members seriously started congratulating David during our sessions. Early on I was still fussing and fighting him on movements that scared me. I still do fuss today (NOBODY wants to do Bird Dog, David.

Nobody.), but in the early days I was a lot louder bc I was truly terrified. I would eventually do the movement after we argued for a while. Apparently we were fractious enough to attract the attention of other members, bc they started approaching us and patting him on the back. One lady was like, *THAT WAS AWESOME!!* I glared at her. He had just made me do some kind of balance and core-building exercise. I was like, *ummmmm…I'm doing all the work here.*

By Year 2 the results were showing enough that strangers approached me individually. They had the opportunity bc I had started using the Locker Room after 1.5 years. In the early days I lacked the mobility and visual confidence to navigate a new space, and I was too embarrassed to ask for help. But now I had several "alone" minutes and all sorts of people would come up to me and say, *I've been watching you for a while. You are doing GREAT. I'd say, My Trainer is David. The man is crazy, but he gets results!!*

By Year 3 people just started watching us bc we are extremely entertaining. There is a ton of bickering. Apparently we thrive on antagonism. LOL. But we actually get a lot of work done, too. I'm writing this in Jan 2018. We started training in November 2013. David got me kicked out of Physical Therapy (*See Vol 2. Learning How to Live – ch. 4 "That Backfired, Didn't It?"*). I was so angry with David for getting me kicked out of the only safe environment I had known since I woke up (Rehab), that I found Coach Randy by March 2014. Coach R is the Golden Child, the one who saved me from having to be alone with Trainer David.

But the *real* Golden Child is Smurfette RD – Jessica – David's wife and my Dietician. But I digress.

David was my springboard into the Thriving stage of Recovery. It started with him. I knew I was transitioning to Medicare as a Disabled Person and what insurance paid for would be limited. So I decided to start building the infrastructure for my long-term Recovery. This is what I learned.

1) <u>**What do you want?**</u>

   Be intentional about this. This is your body, and your life, after all. Make a list of things you want. I do this when looking for anyone to help me – my PCP, massage therapist, different kinds of doctors (although, my PCP is so fabulous I am very happy to just start with her referrals).

   When I hit on the idea of finding a Personal Trainer, this was my list:
   a) Physical Therapy experience
   b) Preferably with Neurological expertise
   c) Female
   d) Close to my house
   e) Optional: like my beloved M37 – 6' tall and blonde

I also verbalized 2 basic Training Goals –
please do this! You need to say what you are
looking for.

f) I want to be taken to the next level of health
g) My situation is different from the norm – is it
okay if I work out in a regular gym like this? If
yes, I will need my Trainer to vouch for my
safety.

2) <u>Identify Targets</u>

Once I knew what I wanted I prayed for God's
guidance, and I got busy on Google. I identified
targets – like if you're looking for a job, or you're
the hiring manager looking for candidates to fill
your position. I made a list of women I wanted to
"interview" to see who was a good fit.

Note: if you have at least one Doc you trust, e.g. a
PCP, ask for referrals!!

3) <u>Interview Them</u>

I set up a "practice" interview at The Gym closest
to my house. It was really a standard sales
appointment, but I had my own agenda. Trainer
David got pulled into that meeting and I explained
what I needed.

I want to be taken to the next level of health…
I need a stronger core for living…

At the mention of core strength, David's gaze

deepened and his head tilted to the side as he rubbed his chin with his thumb and forefinger. He was deep in thought. I ended the session with, *Is there anyone on your team willing to help me?*

David's response was an emphatic, *YES*.

David is obviously not a female former PT. But his confidence and enthusiasm to DO THIS!!! filled the room and as I breathed in the almost palpable excitement I decided that the resonance I felt totally outweighed the things I had written down on my list.

This is something I can't really explain – it was a moment of Recognition – you're either going to know what I'm talking about or you're not, sorry. We recognized each other as kindred spirits during that 15-minute meeting with the Sales rep and my Daddy. I think it was my Core comment that did it. David immediately knew he could help me. And although I had ideas of what I wanted in a Personal Trainer, David's confidence won me over.

David turned out to have a completely nerdy interest in neurological function, so that answered one of my "requirements." And he turned out to be so good he got me kicked out of Physical Therapy. And I got so mad I signed up to try my local AlterG (an anti-gravity treadmill) to learn how to run and prove that my Recovery would not end with formal rehabilitation. I was not looking for anyone else to add to Team Tanimal. But the AlterG came with a Traffic Cop – Randy Rocha – and he would not get out of my way so I could just use the machine.

The wheels in Randy's head were obviously turning when he met me. I do not fit Randy's core client/patient profile, but Randy *knew* he could help me. I was not so sure. I was extremely skeptical bc he had ruined my plan of just getting in the machine to be left alone to recover in peace and I did not regard him kindly in general. There was no moment of Recognition when I met him. But during my second session he opined, *Well, if you want to do this RIGHT…. [you should train with me.]* (see Vol. 3 Learning How to Run – ch. 3)

I was super annoyed at his confidence. *No, Randy, I wanna do this WRONG.* (Sorry, Coach R, but that really is what I thought.) Seriously?!? Who says that kind of thing? And in my world there are 2 rules:
1. Keep your shoes on at all times otherwise you're going to run them over with your wheelchair
2. Avoid the language of Medical Absolutes at *any cost*
Honestly. Who is this guy? Well, once I got over the initial annoyance, I considered the possibility

that Randy might be able to back up the confidence with some results.

Spoiler Alert: He did. The man has the right to say stuff like that and has major street cred for a reason. His personality type leaves no room for brassiness or over-the-top claims of skill. He just makes stony-faced statements of fact born out of personal conviction.

But it took me 3+ years to figure that out. At the time I simply decided to train with him bc although I wasn't looking for anyone else, and I certainly would never have chosen anyone with a background like his (*Sports Medicine – really?*) I was trying to keep my mind open to new ideas. David had been the right choice even though he wasn't what I was looking for. Who's to say it wouldn't happen again?

The point I'm making is that, yes – I just said to know what you want, write it down, and make a list of targets. Absolutely – and approach your list of targets systematically – interview them one by one and see which one is a good fit for you. But keep your mind open to the possibility that what you really *need* might not be on that list.

4) <u>Listen to how people talk</u>
   a) *About competitors:* A year after I met Randy I started looking for another AlterG clinic to add

more running to my week somewhere that was closer to my house. I made my list of targets and started calling around. At one clinic I spoke with the head Therapist/owner who was nice, but then he made a statement about his clinic's competitors that made my hair stand on end. It was a highly critical statement and I just Yessed him to death and hung up the phone as quickly as possible. I was trained to understand that you NEVER say how great your widgets are by saying how everyone else's are inferior. You just play up the positive aspects of your own widgets. Apparently this man never learned this concept. And the way he spoke about his competitors lowered my estimation of him (his clinic, and his own skill level) irreparably. Perhaps my assumptions about him were unfounded, but it doesn't matter. The way he spoke about other people made me unwilling to give him a chance to further disappoint me.

Sorry, that was kind of mean. But I was very upset – I have a much lower tolerance for negativity since I got sick. Anyway, I quickly decided that I'd just add another day with Randy. And then I added a 3rd. Best. Idea. Ever.

b) *How other people talk about your candidate*: Reading someone's resume will give you a quick view of their qualifications. It's superficial, but sometimes it's all you have to go on. Sometimes you can find your person's certifications online – Google all the letters after their name. E.g. MMACS = Mixed Martial Arts Conditioning Specialist. Fascinating, no? Again – this is a completely superficial gauge, but if it's all you have to go on, it's a good starting point. How you REALLY get to know the caliber of your candidate, however, is to observe how other people talk about him/her.

A Therapist at RIO (3rd Hospital) pointed to K3, one of my PT's and said, *We call her The Miracle Worker.* She didn't tell me this herself, her colleagues had given her that title. I heard a woman chat up Coach Randy one day during Stretchy Time – the lady wanted him to rehab her daughter, who had gotten injured at a vital moment in her HS athletic career– Scholarship/Recruiting season. This lady was like, *Oh, Randy, I have read/heard such great things about you....*

And *every time* we train, people just come up to David and ask questions. Members just working out, other Trainers, etc. they all know that D is the one to consult. I later found out that people at Coach Randy's gym (where he is a member, not at the clinic) interrupt his workout to ask questions, too. LOL. Poor Randy. But when my Training with David gets interrupted I breathe a sigh of relief and say, *Take your time!!!* - glad for the extra rest.

5) <u>Signal your intent to work</u>

"I will do WHATEVER my person says to do, as long as (s)he knows what (s)he's doing."

This was one of my statements at my "Interview" at David's Gym. Andy Frankenstein (A6 – the one who taught me to walk) doesn't play around. Working with him made me understand that I respond well to the drill-sergeant type (who is also a nice person.) I knew I was aiming high – I wanted a *very* skilled Trainer, and I was not sure if it were even a reasonable thing for me to ask to work out in a regular gym. So I signaled my intent to work by saying that I have a strong work ethic. However, I was careful to add the caveat that my work ethic would only be deployed in the context of a high level of professional expertise.

I was asking them to give me their best. I figured I'd get a more favorable response if I promised to put my best on the table, too.

6) <u>Look for These 2 Non-negotiable qualities</u>
I told you to keep an open mind to the possibility that you might need something that is not in your

original list of What you Want. However, after having had a completely stellar bunch of Therapists when Insurance funded my Recovery, and since I found David and Randy when I started paying out of pocket, and because I recruited Diahanne the Pool Ninja to help Matt, I've decided that there should are 2 non-negotiable qualities to look for:

a) *Professional Expertise*

Not everyone will grow into a subject-matter expert in his/her field. But given the severity of my injury, it sure made me feel better to know that I was surrounding myself with highly skilled professionals. Sometimes you'll see people at PT who are obviously on their lunch break, or took a couple hours off from work to get their Therapy in. My case is different. I am no longer employed by Corporate America, and am debarred from working bc of what my MRI looks like. Yes, I can sit here and write a book, and do stuff online, but I have built in all sorts of safety measures to make sure I don't aggravate my symptoms. Sometimes it doesn't work bc I just get annoyed and want to do stuff without breaking to squat, stretch, nap, however – but I ALWAYS pay the price.

It was my people who taught me these safety measures, e.g. the 8-minute squat rule (David), the soft-knee stance rule (Randy), and the 20-minute eye stretch rule (Vision Therapy). And because I cannot work in an office anymore, these behaviors are my job. *Learning How to Live* and *Life is My Sport* – the titles of David and Randy's books – are not exaggerations. They are very literal statements on my part. The stakes are high for me – and early on I decided that the skill level of those I asked to help me should be commensurately elevated. I communicated my expectations and signaled that I would be willing to work hard in return. And then I made it my business to make sure my people never regretted that they had chosen to help me.

b) *Emotional Commitment*
...And yes, once you start paying out of pocket, people do in fact *choose* whether or not to help you. There was a lot less choice when I was in traditional insurance-funded, hospital-based care. I was on the roster at the hospital so they kind of *had* to take care of me, and then I went where they told me to go next. Thank the Lord I scored immensely capable and kind professionals when this was how I lived. I received top-notch care above and beyond the call of duty. I got used to it – so when I transitioned to self-funded Recovery I got very intentional about making people opt-in to helping me.

It took a long time, but I realized that in

addition to their superior skill levels, what set David and Randy apart was that they had made an emotional commitment to themselves and to me – that they would help me heal….that they would see this thing through. So when I went looking for a Pool Therapist for Matt Hankey I asked God and then Google, and Diahanne was the first person I called. She actually works from a nursing home in Matt's town so Google suggested it based on geographical proximity.

I chatted with the receptionist – this is another tip – ask the Front Desk for Help!!! Take it from a former administrative professional. We consider it one of our duties to *know people* and to *make connections* to get you the information you need. So after I told the receptionist briefly what I needed, she immediately put me in touch with Diahanne.

I knew from our first conversation that Diahanne's professional credentials are second-to-none. (E.g. she invented the Aqua Jogger decades ago, and when I told her I needed her to teach Matt to walk she didn't bat an eye – she's done this before.) She was more than capable of handling this situation and achieving fantastic results with Matt. But when I showed her my Thank You video and Matt's CARE Channel Video to give her a visual idea of the severity of our injuries, she texted me and I could hear the emotion come through in this one sentence:

I need to get to work.

That was it. I knew from that moment that I didn't need to call anyone else. Not only was she immensely skilled and experienced, she had just made an emotional commitment. Since that day, Diahanne has explained to me that she's a "Mom first, and it shows." She has already raised two sons to manhood and she knows better than anyone else that this is not just about walking.

7) <u>Survivor Loyalty</u>

These are the steps to success....
a) Recognize and Recruit Giftedness
b) Use it to your Advantage
And if you have found someone fabulous to help you
c) Thank the Gifted Person and be loyal to them FOREVER

I refer to this as Survivor Loyalty – I'm not the only one who does this – I've seen other Survivors respond to the help they have received in this way. It's kind of crazy, but what can I say? We are a grateful bunch. And we are smart enough to know that when someone opts-in to help you, you should honor that, especially when you receive the gift of someone who is equipped with specialized knowledge/experience that will help you recover because genius + kindness is a rare and valuable combination. I do not expect everyone to have the skill and compassion that I found – but it's really nice to know that practitioners like David, Randy, and Diahanne exist (See ch. 8 – "The Power of Possibility – a Practitioner Pep Talk).

In my own case, illness has made me see some really ugly parts of life. Ugly Ugly Ugly. *FYI, Ning don't like ugly.* But illness also gave me the opportunity to heal and gave other people the chance to help me. The end result is that I have also seen some terrifyingly beautiful examples of the human experience – rare instances that I wish would become the norm.

My people chose to help me when they didn't have to. People always have a choice. And they said, "Yes." And for that I will be loyal to them forever.

Side Note: Survivor Loyalty benefits accrue to your family (existing and future). Sorry – y'all stuck with me until the day I die. Which, seeing as how I survived the bleed, will likely not be for a very long time.

Ch. 10 Why Survivors Have Body Image Issues

JESSICA SMURFETTE, R.D.

Me: Are you putting your foot down, David?

D: No, you put YOUR foot down when you chose to stop eating food AGAIN!!

Me: (Internal) – *Oh, so this is MY FAULT.*
(External) – Why are you so hangry?!? I gave you a *snack.*

D: Does Randall know about this?

Me: [ambiguous murmuring]

D: ***Does Randall KNOW ABOUT THIS?!?! The answer is "YES" or "NO" !!!!***

Me: [puts nose in the air and turns away] *You see this face, David? This face means* [raises hand palm-out in a blocking gesture for emphasis] *I'm NOT HEARING YOU.*

D: This is the THIRD time we've had this conversation!!! [shakes fist at the ceiling]

Me: (Internal) – *He has a point.*
(External) – Don't you *dare* kick me out of this gym, CUPCAKE.

D: (Pauses to gather strength) Training 3x/week with inadequate nutrition is *wrong.* It will break your body and your mind *down.* I WILL NOT DO IT.

Me: (Internal) *Ohhhhhh – so Sister Maria is trying to take the moral high ground, I see. Whatever. Hmmm…I guess this is not the right time to tell him I'm actually training 4x/week. (I had added another day with Poor Randy so he could rehab my hip.)*

This is an authentic record of the spirited discussion David and I had in November 2016. And yes, it really was the third time he had to call me out on this subject. Jessica is David's wife and serves Team Tanimal as my dietician. Her code name is Smurfette, R.D. She is the one who is in charge. But David (since he sees me a couple times per week and is very sensitive to changes in my wellness) is the one who gets up in my grill in the first place.

I stopped eating food like a normal person in February 2014 due to stress. I was preparing to go to Oregon and my body's first response to stress is loss of appetite and nausea. I got by on two protein shakes a day and a little solid food at lunch – the meal I was likeliest to eat in Daddy's presence. (ROTFLOL – sorry, Daddy xoxo.) I flattered myself that nobody would notice.

Ummmmm.......they noticed. David was the first one to say something, though. At that time he made me keep an exercise log of my workouts and how my body felt. He connected the dots and threw the gauntlet down, citing that he had ironclad evidence that my flagrant violation of the basic rules of alimentation was damaging my body. The situation was complicated by the fact that I had started running in earnest and the Guys had started to train me at a higher level.

The day after David yelled at me I saw Coach R. During Stretchy Time I explained, *You know what the problem is, Randy? That man has TOO MUCH DATA.*

The first time David called me out he indicated that this behavior was unacceptable and I had to take action.

Me: What do you mean?
D: It's time to go see THE PEACOCK.

Me: (Internal) *GASP!! Not THE PEACOCK!!!*

The Peacock is one of Jessica's nicknames (its her former surname). David had told me that his wife was a gifted dietician, and at that time she was also a natural figure competitor (aka bodybuilder). The mere mention of her name was intimidating.

But I saw that David meant business so not only did I go see Jessica, R.D. officially, I joined the concierge medical practice she's based out of bc she recommended my fabulous PCP, and I knew I was ready to pay more for a higher level of care. Side note: super smart decision.

I was THRILLED when I went in for my first consultation and found out that she is not intimidating at all. She is extremely kind and good at what she does. Goal setting and strategizing ensued, and she took the time to educate me on why I should pay attention to certain things.

Side note: I take the Not Intimidating thing back. If I am making a poor health decision she is VERY scary. Completely *terrifying*, actually. She's a petite Tornado of a woman. *See Vol. 2 Learning How to Live – ch. 8 "Smurfette".*

I walked away from that first meeting with a more positive outlook. But I was also like, *Uh oh – my Dietician is married to my Personal Trainer. What a scary combination.*

It turns out that I had to almost *beg* Smurfette to share information with Trainer D bc being the professional that she is, Smurfette observes the rules of Patient Confidentiality scrupulously. But in my case, I knew that information sharing would work in my favor. I'm a HUGE fan of coordinated care.

Still, even though I had Smurfette RD on my side, my eating habits continued to be up and down. After several years of not eating enough (not just a skipped meal here and there), my body rightfully thought I was starving it and started to hold on to EVERYTHING. Plainly stated, when I'm not eating enough I gain weight uncontrollably. David refers to the phenomenon by saying, *You're in storage mode (again).*

We have made progress, but also had some...consistency issues. (see *Vol. 2 Learning How to Live – ch. 9 "No One Asked You."*)

And the fact that I'm even writing this chapter is a Flagrant Violation of MHP's Rule – I'm not supposed to talk about Size, Shape, Weight, or Food. She made this rule for my own sanity. (She treats Eating Disorders, too, although I'm really thankful not to have one.) At this point I've heard every single POV and she instituted the rule to help me leave this matter in the hands of the professionals (particularly Smurfette).

To be clear, I have PLENTY of resources. Not only do I have Smurfette, RD, I have an entire team of medical professionals ready to assist me.

One day at the end of 2016, Randy kindly offered, *Let me know if you want me to attack your body fat.*

ROTFLOL! I was like, *Erm, thanks, but no, I'm all set. Cheers.* I did ask him to define "attack your body fat" and it involved the use of a food diary, the body fat scale he uses to certify wrestlers, and the training techniques he'd choose accordingly.

The offer itself was a genuine offer to help – I just think Randy's word choice was hilariously characteristic. To a mind like his if there's a problem we will ATTACK it. But he was very careful to hedge his offer of help with well-chosen language about how he did not acknowledge that there was an issue, he just knew I was concerned about it and wanted to help out if he could. While I couldn't help smirking a little at the incident, I appreciated the offer all the same.

The last time this happened David made me tell him how many times I was eating a day. When I just murmured evasively he was like, *Ok, FINE. We're going to backtrack. You're not ready for counting calories and macros in My Fitness Pal. For now I want you to concentrate on eating 3 meals a day.*

Oh, good, I thought. *My Fitness Pal broke up with me a long time ago, anyway.* It went without saying that my meals should be whole-food and nutrient dense. And when I made my medical rounds, Smurfette RD said that the 3 meals a day thing was a good goal. My PCP also supported this approach. And when I told my lovely Neurologist the whole saga she said, *It's not a fight. David's trying to help you.*

Me: (Internal) False. It's *always* a fight.

You will notice that I'm just sitting here telling you funny stories about how difficult I am to deal with. I named this chapter "Why Survivors Have Body Image Issues" for a reason. I thought that "Smurfette is trying to kill me" might not be as funny to the public as I think it is. But the bottom line I that I have no idea on how to conquer body image issues – I'm not equipped to talk about that subject. But I have observed that most of my Survivor Friends have body image issues, and I want to explain why.

Survivors have body image issues bc our bodies are different than they used to be. What I used to look like doesn't matter. It is completely immaterial that people tell me that I look very similar to my pre-AVM self. Because to me, it's different. Everything feels different, and to my eyes, *looks* different.

And when people say (I'm talking about people in general, NOT Smurfette, bc she's never said this), *Well you know, it's natural that the body will change as you age,* this is a true statement but it is just another piece of bad news to me (and probably many other survivors) as opposed to the healthy readjustment of expectations that the general population undergoes when they realize they are getting older. Aging is a natural part of life. However, I am unable to experience most of the benefits of aging because I got sick. True, I've learned a lot as I've gotten older, hence this book. But the family and career milestones my peers have celebrated as part of the normal course of human social development are not my experience. I'm not saying that "You're getting older," is not true and that you shouldn't say this. I'm saying that there are complicating factors I must deal with that make the challenge of aging gracefully more problematic on multiple levels. It's still difficult to accept 100% of the ramifications of my illness with cloudless peace.

What is comforting, however, is that I found out that I'm not the only one who thinks like this. I've met Survivors of all ages, genders, ethnicities, etc. who struggle with the same issues I do.

And to a Survivor with disabilities that limit every day activities there are a lot of issues to deal with when taking charge of your nutrition. You have to budget your finances to eat the food you want, but you also have to have the stamina and kitchen mobility to cook it, go pick it up if you use a meal service, (or ask someone else to do these activities) and the storage space in the fridge if you live with others. And News Flash: if you have children your instinct will be to prioritize feeding them and helping them with their homework. If you lack the energy to "do it all" – the person who gets moved to the bottom of the list is usually going to be you.

So, yeah – there are a lot of moving parts here, and I'm obviously still working on this issue. But I've made a lot of progress! I've found solutions (over 3+ years) to many of the challenges I just listed. David and Randy built me up so I don't have to sit down every 5 minutes in the kitchen (I used to literally set a timer). Other Survivors gave me tips on how to cook Disabled-style (e.g. how to plan a meal and stay safe). I bought a Vitamix bc it's super powerful and the blade is not detachable, so I felt safer. I signed up for a Meal Preparation service to supplement my own cooking.

Side note: I am the daughter of Baker Smurf. My Mommy is SUCH a good cook. Ask anyone. But I have so much food-related baggage (much of it related to having a PEG in the hospital) I am more comfortable eating the style of food I prepare myself. But don't get me wrong – if she makes laksa, I'm THERE. (Once I heat up my shirataki noodles.)

Anyway, if you're reading this and you're not comfortable in your own skin – take heart you're not the only one.

And Smurfette, thank you for sticking with me.

Ch. 11 The Measure of Success
WHY NUMBERS DO NOT DEFINE YOU (BUT THEY CAN HELP TRACK YOUR PROGRESS)

How often and in what manner do you measure success?

That was the first question I asked before starting Vision Therapy. There is a VT clinic very near my house and I was already familiar with them bc I had gotten routine eye exams there prior to moving to Oregon. After my bleed they were the obvious choice for my first post-AVM checkup. I went in for new prescriptions for contacts and glasses, but they knew they could help me and explained Vision Therapy to me.

Before I made any decisions, my doc charged me to go do my research. I liked that – no pressure, just helpful information and a charge to go do my homework. I started researching and I found out that there are a plurality of opinions on Vision Therapy, but I was intrigued by the idea of it. My eyes had never worked normally, granted (I have amblyopia – a lazy eye), but this is what saved me from the double vision many people suffer after an injury like mine. I never used both eyes, anyway – I was used to blocking the information from one eye out.

But the challenge now would be to take my new set of physical parameters – my injury had changed my vision so much that I just kept my eyes down or shut them entirely so I wouldn't have to deal with all the crazy movement – and to train my brain to use my eyes in a new way for my New Life.

Here is an old Blog Post from Learning How... (blog.annninglearninghow.com – or go to ShreddedGrace.com→media→blog)

149. Why I Choose Therapy..and trust the Pros to help me Recover

blog.annninglearninghow.com
published 4.15.2013

When I first starting going to The Place (ARHM, my first outpatient rehab hospital) I was still getting accustomed to RecoveryLand's layout and it was so early in my treatment there that I hadn't yet been paired up with A (6). So I asked E (PT10) if I would just get better in time and why I had to do therapy.

Well, she said, it's likely you're going to heal with time, but until then...[what do you do?]

1. Therapy is about living life.

As I prepared to be discharged from The Place after ~6 months, I had major anxiety over getting **"kicked out."** A (6) explained to me that there was nothing to be nervous about; the idea was that I'd eventually return, and that therapy is about learning to live life. I didn't take the "living life" concept seriously until I really thought about it for months after, and he was right. (*Side*

note: I __hate it__ when A's right! I said that to Mom in the parking lot after receiving another medical vote for a recovery that would be less than 100%. Okay, fine. Let's go for 99.9...I extrapolated this idea from a convo with Je. PS. Props to docs who have to say unpopular things.)
It's true in that I practice what I learned in therapy as I sit in a chair, eat a meal, type this at my computer, and basically, while I do everything else when I'm awake. Yes, I learned how to sit on a mat in the gym, and how to get up from the gym floor if I had a fall, but I sit, fall, and get up in the real world. And I go to the store and eat at restaurants and climb the stairs at church.

What E said to me was absolutely on target in a thought-provoking way. Maybe I would get better by just waiting this thing out. But in the meantime I still want to get my own cup of water when I'm thirsty, and venture out into the community. So I've learned the skills that help me to do what I want to do in the real world by practicing them in a controlled environment under the supervision of **licensed professionals**. There's also a huge achievement factor in RecoveryLand – you have to set goals in therapy, and the point is to figure out ways to reach them, even if it takes a while. Progress is closely monitored and systematically measured so you can tell if you need to adjust your strategy, or if your plan of attack is proving to be effective, it's easy to celebrate.

2. I'd rather be doing something (even if it doesn't work) than nothing.

Have you seen my **medical disclaimer** (click on the link and scroll down)? I really do stand by that – e.g. there is a school of thought that says, I love Vision Therapy – there's no other way to train the brain to "see" the best way your eyes can see. There's another school of thought that simply says, I don't believe in that – that doesn't work. Reading is difficult for me at present, but when my Eye Doc told me to go home and research VT before deciding to go this route it took me two seconds to understand that this course of treatment is a source of debate, although I have chosen to immerse myself in an environment of pro-VTers. So yeah – everyone needs to do his/her homework and decide what the best course of treatment is for him/her.

At my next appointment I told my Eye Doc, I'd rather do this even if it doesn't work than nothing. I'm ignoring the question of "does it work?" at the moment and just saying, Seriously? Sitting on your hands and hoping for the best is an option? Well, it's a bad option, IMHO. *(Side note: Remember that my condition is in flux. I am not referring to dealing with a permanent condition. Learning to live wheelchair or prosthetic-style = huge heavy lifting.)* I'm NOT saying, God helps those who help themselves (that is not scriptural, BTW), I'm just saying that my personality does not lend itself to inaction. I need the idea of goal-setting and a professional to break achievement into baby steps.
So I chose VT with a well-rounded view of the discipline, and I was encouraged to pursue the necessary research by my VT Practice, and I recommend research to you as a good course of action before pursuing any kind of treatment.

Admittedly, I chose acupuncture with somewhat less (okay, zero) research. I just went to CMD based on my Uncle/Aunt's recommendation, and the vague knowledge that Chinese people having been doing this sort of thing for a long time and people all over the world love acupuncture, so I wanted to try it, especially since I had nothing to lose. Like I told CMD on day 1, my primary goal is pain relief (check! Goal met), any other relief I can get from her ministrations I will treat as a welcome surprise.

3.   Therapy and Alternative Medicine have changed the way I live

I'm still ignoring the "does it work?" question. Well, let me list the following items – these may be interpreted either as improvement due to treatment or coincidence, depending on your persuasion:

a. Vision: My neurologist saw me 3-4 months after I started VT. I had not seen her since starting treatment. She immediately noticed that I was using my eyes to look at her while talking in a way I had not been able to before, and that my nstagmus (jumpy eyes) had improved (except when looking up).

b. Vision: My tests (e.g. those crazy looking space goggles) indicate my left eye is "waking up" – meaning that I am using my eyes in a way I was unable to pre-injury.

c. CM: The only relief I'm willing to state emphatically (since I'm naturally **tentative** about these things) is that I have much less pain in my left side since starting to see CMD. Other things I'm still processing but have happily noticed: greater mobility in the right (weaker) side of my face, more freedom of movement in my left hip, overall improvement in my gait.

...

I wrote the blog post above in April 2013. Almost 5 years have passed.

1. Ninja CMD made me a HUGE believer in the efficacy of acupuncture and TCM in general. She is a kind and compassionate practitioner. She's the reason I was able to start exercising more and she was the first person EVER to give me an open-ended promise of help. See Vol. 2 – *Learning How to Live* ch. 5 "Expect More".

197

2. I Spent a couple years in VT but was discharged several years ago. I returned in Dec 2017 for a new Rx for my contacts. I forgot how tiring vision tasks are – because I was a VT patient I didn't just get an eye exam, I got the full battery of tests. And they revealed that I had not regressed in the years since I was in VT twice a week. I am still using my eyes better than ever.

It's true, you know – EVERYONE has noticed. I use my eyes completely differently than when I was first injured, and Boo Boo informed me in 2014-15 that I was using them both at once more than I ever did before my AVM rupture. But still, I like more formal ways of testing – that's why I had asked my doc, "How often and in what manner do you measure success?"

Most of my Rehab Hospitals had monthly evaluations in PT – you had to do all these different tests and they either counted the number of reps you could do within X seconds, or measured your success with a tape measure, etc. So I asked my Vision Therapy clinic how they planned on gauging my success. Well – it turns out they have A LOT of tests to measure your progress. And I *did* progress under the watchful eye of my doc in the Therapy room, and in the company of several wonderful VT helpers who were in school to study this sort of thing, and alongside fellow patients – many of whom were hilarious children who kept me laughing while I tried desperately to achieve binocularity.

Vision Therapy worked for me. Like I say above, and like they told me – go do your research and make your own decision. But add this data point: VT changed the way I approach life. I'm sitting here writing this book bc I have been trained in how to deploy and stretch my visual capital wisely. Yes, I have screen set to ZOOM really big, but hey – this is working out pretty well bc I know how to use my eyes in a healthy way.

I still cannot read "normally" but it's gotten a LOT better. I will never forget the day I realized it was easier to read. I was a voracious reader as a child. That's how I learned to write – I read a lot. Anyway, Mommy, I never told you, but on the day I realized it was easier to read I stayed up until 3am reading on my Kindle. (It was a book M37 had recommended.) A Kindle, or my phone, is easier to hold than a book, and I use the option where you can make the screen black and the font white.

Yes, it's a lot easier to read, but I still save my visual bullets carefully for when I *really* need them. I prefer audiobooks (or my device's text-to-speech function when available), and pretend to play the piano by ear now (do you know how many hymns you can play in C? LOL). But if I really need to read something important, I can. But I have obliging friends who help me out – e.g. one day I asked David to fix my arm. He was going to put some arnica gel on my forearm but I was like, WAIT!! I'm ALLERGIC! (one of the post-AVM complications) But I couldn't remember the name of the thing I'm allergic to. So D sat there and read the *entire* ingredient list. It was fine, so he fixed my arm and we trained as usual. See? We do have some moments of harmony.

So all this is to say that there SHOULD be a methodical way in which your people measure your progress. I am a HUGE proponent of goal setting. I like everyone to know the goal so we can pursue it together and remain on track. If you would like me to make a PowerPoint slide, I will gladly do so.

Even if you *don't* want me to make a PowerPoint slide, I will email you one later. But I'm gonna PDF it bc I don't like people messing with my files. As Kim says, *Lock it down.* ROTFLOL. Man alive, I miss Corporate America.

Hey, Randy – sorry about that time (ok, ALL the times) Bossy Smurf stole your lunch money. Sorry, to you, too, David.

Just kidding. #noregrets

While I advocate the clear communication of goals, (I think in B-school we learned that these goals should be Actionable, Measureable, Time-Bound, and I forget what else), in Recoveryland it is crucial to not let the NUMBERS get in the way of seeing the PERSON. Example:

Soon after I had convinced Matt Hankey to let me work with him, but before I had found Diahanne the Pool Ninja I got an SOS email from him one night. It had been a discouraging day in Recoveryland for him. I could hear the disappointment in his voice.

Abort mission, Ann – we can't do this.

He had gone to PT at the hospital that day and been informed that he had been approved for 8 sessions.

8 sessions? When I learned how to walk this would have lasted me less than 3 weeks.

I was immediately up in arms. Sorry for sounding mean, Matt, but I was upset.

I am aborting NOTHING. That is not how this is going to work. I've done this before, Matt – let me explain how it works: They HAVE to be able to justify to the insurance company that you are making progress and that they (Insurance) should keep on paying for Therapy for you. So what's gonna happen is that your PT's are gonna take their little clipboards out and measure you WITHIN an INCH of your life – but Matt, you listen up –

THOSE NUMBERS
DO.
NOT.
DEFINE.
YOU.

Matt had been in a power chair for almost 5 years. He had not had the access to care that would have helped him early on. I knew it was highly unlikely that the his visits to the outpatient clinic would yield numbers that would wow the Insurance Company enough to justify the amount of dedicated care he required. I could not bear the thought that he would fall into the trap of thinking that those numbers were a definitive portrait of his Recovery.

I had zero insight into what was happening at Matt's PT sessions. Matt lives in Oregon – we did not know each other prior to injury, we just became friends at our support group, AVMSurvivors.org. But what I DID know about Matt was this: He was doing what he could with what he had. What did he have? Really fantastic pictures and videos of him skateboarding. It must have ripped his heart out every time he uploaded something to Facebook. But he did it anyway bc as a Survivor, he was building his base.

That behavior alone told me that Matt had the courage to Reach Higher.

But then he told me that it wasn't weird that I thought those things about the Valley – that I wasn't the only one.

SNIFF.

Mm hmmm....Yeah.

Side note: my underlying message to Matt all this time has been that I'd still want to be his friend even if he never walked again. His value as a person is COMPLETELY INDEPENDENT of physical achievement. That said, I am a Tan. Plus I went to school for this – you never ever leave money on the table. NEVER. EVER. If there's an opportunity in front of you, use it up.

Let me state for the record: My former employer took GREAT care of me when I got sick. I had fantastic insurance. The people at my hospitals were compassionate and very skilled professionals who (after saving my life) taught me to sit, stand, eat, talk, and walk. I will always be grateful for what they did for me.

But some cases develop in a way that our healthcare system is not intended to accommodate. That's just how it is. It had happened to me – everything that is pushing me forward in my Recovery now is self-funded. And that's why I was like, *Matt's gonna get crushed by the machinery of a system that can simply not support the level of care he needs. I can't just sit here and let that happen.* Measurements are a good, healthy way to check on if your system is working. But please never lose sight of the fact that the most important indicators of personal value cannot be recorded as a number.

Ch. 12 The Bossy and Sassy Show
HOW TO CHOOSE A MEDICAL ID
MEGAN

Jason's not going to let us go to Vegas now, is he?

I had just done something that would NOT increase Coach J's confidence in letting Megan and me hang out in a new city by ourselves....or probably under adult supervision, either. But whatever.

I assure you that Megan and I are both adults. However, we both have significant brain injuries. Jason is Megan's husband. She is the first friend God gave me after I got sick. This is how we met:

The Rehabilitation Institute of Oregon (RIO – my 3rd Hospital, Megan's 2nd) May/June 2011

I arrived at RIO the week before Megan. She moved in after her car was run over by a truck while she was driving to work. We refer to this incident simply as "The Wreck."

It was Very. Very. BAD.

But I had no notion of this while we were hospitalized. I just saw that
1. She had pretty hair – long, brown, and curly
2. She wore STREET CLOTHES. (The nurses gave me scrub pants and a jacket, and I wore the

same 3 T-shirts in rotation. 2 of them had been purchased by Mom at Target the week before bc I had no rehab clothes and at RIO patients did not wear hospital gowns.) I was *not amused* to see Megan with her pretty hair and fashionable outfits. But I could not deny that Megan looked super cute, and that just annoyed me. XOXOXO just being honest, Sassy.

3. She did NORMAL things, e.g. she'd put on hand lotion and sip coffee while in the waiting room between rehab sessions. For some reason this really grieved me. It hurt my feelings a lot bc they were very mundane things, but they were actions that seemed to belong to another way of life that I desperately wanted to rejoin.

And THEN, the icing on the cake was that even though the girl had arrived an *entire week* after me she was cruising around with her single point cane after a month while I watched glumly from my wheelchair. I don't think we've ever discussed this. Man alive, I was entirely *consumed* with envy. I mean, we were both in wheelchairs. But in the space of a month she was gliding effortlessly around the "RIO Loop," with the cane barely touching the floor.

My friends Kim and Joyce, who had flown to Oregon to MD to visit me bc they are SO NICE have since informed me that they remember Megan, and she had stitches *all over*. Yes, she was walking, but she was doing so with a new hip and a huge rod in her arm, not to mention the things that had happened to her brain. Her body had been very much broken by The Wreck, but the fractures in her skull relieved some of the swelling in her brain. I did not understand this, but the natures of our injuries are very different. So yes, she walked faster than I did, but she explained to me later that she was MUCH less lucid.

So I just observed her from a distance during that month. And saw that she was shadowed by her husband, Jason, and her Mom and Dad were always there, too. Jason and Megan's Dad were the witnesses on my Court Documents, and I had no idea the little blonde lady sitting next to Megan's chair or bed was actually her *mother*.

I observed and was not amused. To be clear, I was not amused by *anything* at that point – I was convinced that I was stuck in a dream and was trying desperately to wake up. After a couple weeks of growing lucidity, however, I decided that if God wanted me to wake up, I'd wake up, so I stopped trying so hard. However, I then decided that if this situation were not a dream, well then I was CLEARLY trapped in a Very Bad Reality TV show or a super scary video game. (PS. Our Neuropsych was fascinated by my Reality TV show theory. He was like, *Tell me more about this TV show*. Me: *Not much to be said, really*

– insert emoji with slit eyes.)   And then, near the end of my stay I decided that in order to advance to the next level in this horrifying video game I had to do activities that I used to do in my Old Life.

At the top of my list was "Visit Sick People in the Hospital." Mommy had pointed out Megan's room to me earlier that day. She was laboring under the delusion that since we were the same age whereas everyone else in rehab was 30-50 years older, that we had become instant friends. So I waited until Mommy Daddy had gone home for the night and I set about my Visitation rounds. I had a couple nurses I wanted to find and talk to, and there was one other patient I wanted to visit in addition to Megan. By that time I was supremely proud of myself for having learned to manipulate my wheelchair independently. I still didn't do it overly well, but I could go places. So I wheeled myself to Megan's room. She was in bed, and Jason was chatting quietly with her.

That was the first (and only) time I spoke directly to her. In that moment, all animosity faded away because she was just *so nice.* I understand now that she was still very confused. So was I – I mean, I only went to visit them so I could advance to the next level in my Video Game – but her confusion was a lot sweeter than mine. She just greeted me shyly, and told me what kind of work she did in a sweetly timorous little voice.

Jason let us talk. I mean, what was the poor guy supposed to do? He ascertained that I was a rather unusual specimen, but was probably harmless, so we just introduced ourselves like regular people do – *What's your name, where do you live, what do you do, etc?* Jason and Megan, THANK YOU for not throwing me out of your room. You guys are really nice. Because if the tables had been turned I would not have hesitated to press the red call button to summon a nurse to eject you immediately.

I was discharged a few days later. And no, I did not reach the next level of the video game – it turns out the situation really WAS reality. Megan went home a week later. And for 2 years we recovered on separate coasts – I had moved to the Washington, D.C. area, and she moved back to her house in Oregon. Maybe 2 weeks after Mommy and Daddy flew me to the house I grew up in, I was lying in my bed downstairs (they made me a bed in the library and the only thing I was allowed to do unsupervised was look at the ceiling), and Daddy came to tell me, *I got an email from [Megan's Dad]. She still asks for you.*

SNIFF. I don't know why, but I cried right then and there. I was lying in my bed and I tried to use Ed Blueberry to cover my face so Daddy wouldn't see my tears. *Tell her "hi" for me and that I hope she doesn't hurt anymore.*

I could only say those few words and fondly hoped Daddy would walk away so I could cry in peace. *Why was I crying?* I gave myself a mental shake. *Sheesh. I barely LIKED the girl.*

LOL. Yeah, the rosy feeling of comradeship born out of our one meeting had faded. But if you have been in a situation like ours, you know that Survivorship is so isolating. I was still working through what had happened and had very strong and emotionally raw memories of RIO – that was the place I woke up in earnest. That was the place where Mommy had told me that yes, this had really happened. That was the place I learned that I had lost everything and I'd never see my home again. But Megan had been there. She would *understand.*

During those two years I thought of her *all the time.* We had extensive conversations in my head. And she and Jason made it into my first book (Vol. 1) *Learning How….to Walk and Wait.* I reasoned within myself that publishing a book was a good milestone to use as a reason to find and contact her. I would get on Google and figure that out once I published that book.

But 6 months prior to publishing – *PING!* – I got an email. *"It's me, Megan. We were at RIO together. Do you remember?"*

I was still in bed that morning. I read the first line of her email on my phone and cast it aside as I burst into tears. MEGAN!! OF COURSE I remember you!!

Sniff Sniff Sniff.

SOB SOB, intermittent Ugly Crying…

[I can't even talk about this. I have to go downstairs. ERKEP is here. I will be right back
…
3 hours later…
I'm back!!.]

So then I wrote an email to Megan that was soooooo long.

And I explained, *I assumed that this was the only email I'd ever write you. And I had a lot to say – I was talking to you in my head for two years.*

Explanation: I assumed that this was the only email I'd write to Megan bc this had become common in my post-injury life. What I had erroneously thought was a reconnection or a continuance of a relationship was actually a goodbye. I understand now that this was a very natural thing to occur in the ebb and flow of life. However, I did not fully understand the implications of my injury and my geographical removal from my Old Life. I had also tried to reach out and make some connections in Survivor Land but had come up empty-handed. At that point I was simply not equipped to understand these events, so I just made a blanket rule to protect myself emotionally. Matt Hankey summarized it with elegant terseness after I gave him a long pep talk about risk taking and finding the right kind of help for recovery. I went on for several paragraphs via email. He (typing with one finger) wrote back, *I get it, I get it: EXPECT NOTHING.*

But out of all the people in the world, Megan is the one I shouldn't have worried about disappearing. It's been over 5 years. She's still around. And we can text each other like, *Blah blah blah* and it's ALWAYS relevant, funny, and encouraging. We are bound by a unique experience – by both trauma and the fact that we both started to heal in the same environment.

Our relationship has flourished by both private digital correspondence and on public comments on social media. Our mothers would read these comments and say, *They are SO ALIKE.* It really is kind of scary. I mean – our personalities are remarkably alike, and our writing voices are similar. We both had reputations for being nice people before we got sick, and then TBI did something to our social filters. She was the first one to verbalize this to me in a hilarious text string in which she explained what had happened that day at the pharmacy. Except she'd say, *So I told the pharmacist, ABC…but then SASSY MEGAN said in my head, XYZ.*

ROTFLOL! That's why I call her Sassy Smurf. Even her Sassy voice is soooo sweet. We met lucidly for the first time in 2014 when I returned to OR to dispose of my earthly belongings (see Randy's book, *Vol. 3 – Learning How to Run: Life is my Sport, ch. 8 "The Full Workout"*). I was dreading that trip and – ooh! I just remembered this – Megan sent me a message saying she was nervous to meet me in person. I was like, *Girl – you are the ONLY thing I'm looking forward to.*

That was completely true. It was an emotionally grueling prospect – I had seriously tried to convince Mommy Daddy to send me to Boo Boo's house while they snuck into Oregon, gave all my things away to the Salvation Army, and snuck back out, but Mommy refused. She said that it would be a good and healthy thing if I faced everything. Which it was. Crazy and gut-wrenching, but I'm glad I did it. I made appointments with significant doctors and nurses, and visited all 3 Hospitals. I had a "Hello" Party for my former Intel colleagues because I stopped saying "Goodbye" after I left RIO. I just couldn't do it anymore.

But I looked forward to seeing Megan with unclouded anticipation. I wasn't overly nervous – she was naturally a little unsure – I feel it too, it comes with the TBI territory. There are a lot of reasons for us to feel unsure of ourselves. Sometimes we misremember things, and/or get confused bc life has been so "exciting."

I was not disappointed. We saw Megan and Jason for dinner one night and then she and her Mom drove over the next day for a fro yo date with Mommy and me. Megan held my hand so I wouldn't trip and got my fro yo for me. While we were choosing our flavors I glanced over and saw our mothers deep in conversation at the table.

Megan, LOOK - I hissed to her over the toppings bar, nodding my head in the direction of our mothers, *They are **commiserating**!!*

ROTFLOL. They totally *were*, FYI. There was a point at RIO when my mom started following me around during Therapy apologizing to the Therapists for the crazy things I'd say. Mommy was also appalled to watch me learn how to groom myself without standing at a sink. I'd try to wash my face with a washcloth while seated in my wheelchair and Mommy was like, *WHAT ARE YOU DOING?!?!?* She thought I was rubbing too hard.

Megan's mom had a similarly difficult situation on her hands. Megan and I were grown women at the time of our injuries. We were not used to being assisted with grooming activities. But Megan's mom is a neuro nurse and it was *especially* painful for her to watch her daughter casually run a comb through her

214

hair and barely touch her teeth with a brush and proclaim triumphantly, *All done!!*

So, yeah – our mothers had A LOT to talk about. And they continued to say how alike we are. The other things we learned on that trip were:

(1) Jason really IS as nice as he was in a hospital. We all knew it just by observing him at RIO. But when we got to share a meal and talk for real after 2 years of Recovery, we all agreed that the man is a Rockstar.

(2) Megan is A LOT nicer than I am. I drew this conclusion based on taking mental notes on her verbal patterns and overall demeanor for two days. After the trip I told Mommy my hypothesis, *I think Megan is a lot nicer than I am.* Mommy TOTALLY agreed.

Based on our interactions, digital and in person, we thought it unlikely that would be overly helpful for us to live in the same town and have direct access to each other all the time. Our sense of Survivor humor is so similar that we'd likely just egg each other on in our naughtiness. But it's not *all* naughty. I think she has impressive powers of imagination – example: she has totally bought in to my Video Game idea and added these details:

- We have secret powers and lots of obstacles in our paths

- Although we do not have unlimited lives we CAN come back from very low energy/battery power states
- We have strength in numbers and can use each other to enhance our abilities, e.g jumping higher by tossing one another, leapfrogging, finding super strength when hands are joined to block enemies

When I said, *Jason's not going to let us go to Vegas now, is he?*

Megan was like, *LOL. Ummm, no. Vegas, what?!!*

Me: *Wait – did I not tell you we were supposed to go to Vegas?!?! We have this TV program in my head called* The Bossy and Sassy Show. *It's a documentary. The Vegas episode was going to be our Christmas special.*

(Side note: I call myself Bossy Smurf. This tendency was born out of my first job, which was as an administrative assistant. I ran a tight ship and retain a preference for certain calendar protocols and communication conventions. I realized right away that I would not be able to bend David/Randy to my will. But that has not stopped me getting all Bossy Smurf on both of them!! It's for their own good – I promise [wink,wink].)

She laughed and indicated that I had not mentioned this to her. Which is HILARIOUS in and of itself bc it's one of the brain-injured behaviors we both present. We're never quite sure if this or that really happened, or if that conversation actually took place or if we just imagined it.

NOW I remember – I actually told Coach Randy that Megan and I were going to Vegas. He thought it was a GREAT idea. I talked about it with him – that's why I thought I had already discussed it with Megan.

ANYWAY, even though Megan and I will not likely be going to Vegas, or anywhere else anytime soon (travel is difficult for me, and even short plane rides do things to my legs and head), if I *could,* I'd fly straight into PDX and inform Megan, *I'm gonna be here for a month. Start talking.*

I have avoided talking about the details of our friendship for several years. Frankly, it was too weird for me – it was shocking that God would be so *kind* to me. He knew that I would wake up in the hospital EXTREMELY trust-averse. I woke up looking for a fight. And when the nurses really do try to wake you up they do it by hurting you. My family said they were always extremely apologetic, but they HAD to do it. I actually remember – there were a lot of kind, encouraging words accompanied by extremely aggressive pinching. Like the kind that will leave bruises. But they have to go to extreme measures bc the patient is, after all, "asleep."

The nurses are looking for you to "Respond" – a *reflexive* response, like if you twitch, is good, but a *defensive* response, like if you try to block them, is better bc it shows a higher level of brain function. So from the get go, I was thinking, I need to defend myself.

Megan's mom explained that the First Responders had told her that Megan had been "combative" when they extracted her from the vehicle. And these were not strangers – they knew Megan bc they were based out of the clinic where Megan worked as a PA. You can imagine that their hearts were breaking as they took her out of The Wreck and got her on the chopper. But Megan, with a crushed body and a consciousness unaware, was running on some kind of lower-level instinct that told her to FIGHT.

Her mom, as a neuro nurse, knew that this combativeness was a strong indicator of brain injury.

Sniff sniff sniff.

But the only reason why I can talk about this is bc Megan lived and is now the Sassiest Smurf EVER and my sweet sister.

But at the time of our injuries, we both woke up with fists raised, ready to engage at the slightest provocation. When no one was around to fight, however, Megan was plenty rowdy on her own. She ripped her sutures out with her teeth one day when she was still supposed to be unconscious enough to get an MRI. You're supposed to be still while in the tube. Yeah, that didn't work out. Megan totally messed up the image in addition to her stitches. They also had to tent her bed once she made it to RIO. Yes, she was dealing with awful new physical parameters, but the nurses knew they still had to take preventative measures bc they had a live one on their hands.

I did not admit the fact that I'm spoiling for a fight until I met David and Randy and was COMPLETELY annoyed by their attempts (well-meaning, gentlemanly efforts) to be nice to me. Homey don't play ANY o' dat.

God knew that I would wake up so unwilling to entertain the idea of friendship bc I had lost my old life and was not up for opening myself up for more hurt, that He'd have to approach me very carefully. So he gave me a gentle, funny friend in the hospital who experienced things I thought I was the only one who'd remember. It occurred to me, maybe after a year, that Megan would understand the ache I carried in my heart, especially when I remembered those early days. And I wanted so desperately to find her and talk to her – I gave myself a schedule – like I said, when I published my first book, I'd make an effort to find her. But then 6 months ahead of schedule, before I had even had a chance to formulate my desire to contact Megan into a prayer request, God brought her to ME. Her next-door neighbors "happened" to be my friends from church. They compared notes and realized that we had been at RIO at the same time.

In the end I didn't have to lift a finger.

The main thing, though, is that I was not scared of Megan. It makes me think about how God approached mankind. God, being you know, *God*, has every right to rule and to reign. But when He decided how to have a relationship with humankind, He did not come as a conquering King. He chose to come as a baby in a manger. Nobody's going to be scared of a baby. A baby needs to be *held*. We do that by instinct.

When discussing my faith I hasten to point out that God gave me no special knowledge while I was in The Valley of the Shadow of Death. There was no divine revelation, and after I woke up there was no writing in the sky, although I'm not gonna lie, that would have been pretty cool and unmistakable. But what God did instead was to make me capable of evaluating my beliefs using simple logic and publicly available information, and then he sent me some lightning bolts of encouragement to make me feel really special.

Megan was the first lightning bolt, but she came in a totally non-scary package that was exactly like me, except nicer. I'm never going to get over the miracle of our friendship. And then, as we both have recovered in different ways, what happened next was both appalling and thrilling to watch.

Megan fought hard to win back her PA license and return to work. And then in Feb 2016, she had a grand mal seizure while running. She was found lying on a road. Thank God that a vehicle stopped and summoned help. Megan woke up in the ambulance and was unable to use words to give the EMT's any information.

Ummmm....trauma?!?! First of all, we have the whole waking up in the ambulance thing. If this has ever happened to you, you know that once is enough. Technically, I think she was transported by air that first time, but you know what I mean. Second of all, there is the sensation of being unable to produce speech to communicate. That is TERRIFYING.

And all this happened a couple weeks after she returned home from Rwanda, where she had gone on medical missions. I'm completely serious. She survived The Wreck, learned how to walk and use her limbs again, got relicensed, and joined a team going to Africa to serve the poor with their medical expertise. And then this seizure happened and her privileges got revoked – no work, no driving, basically no independence – she was being watched by her family because there was no good medical reason why this episode occurred, there was no way to predict another, so they needed to protect her.

The next one happened a year later in February 2017. It was another grand mal seizure, but this time she was in the house – in a vacation rental with her family. They heard a thud in the kitchen and went to investigate. It was Megan falling on the floor. Thankfully, many of her family members are first responders and/or medical professionals, so they knew what to do. (After they turned the gas stove off – she had inadvertently switched the nob on with her head in her descent.) Jason was working at the time, but drove down immediately to be with her. Poor guy. Sniff.

So again – Megan had regained the privileges of driving and working, and general independence. With each month that passed seizure-free, she had more liberty to live. But it all came to a screeching halt in February 2017 – again, the tests revealed zero helpful information on why this had happened, or when it might occur again in the future. I was so sad for her. I had gone through the process in one fell swoop in 2011. But her seizures were 5 and 6 years AFTER The Wreck, after she had successfully regained so much. Now her privileges were being revoked. For me it had been a clean break. My friend Megan was suffering a much longer, slower, goodbye.

And THEN what did she do? In September 2017 she flew to Texas with a team to do Hurricane Harvey Relief – the kind where you clean out flooded, fetid houses and put the piles on the street hoping the FEMA truck will come soon. Megan could no longer work, but Jason agreed that she was well enough to go help out. Megan was a gymnast at Oregon State and he was a wrestler at the University of Oregon. The fierceness of competitive sport has stayed with them. That's why I call Jason, "Coach J" – he's my *other* favorite wrestling coach. (He coaches wrestling at the high school where he teaches.)

And despite the physical trauma and metal implants in her body, Megan has retained the agility and strength of a Division I athlete. I know bc I heard the PT's discussing her at RIO one day. She was an asset to her team in Texas – her work ethic and stamina command respect. And when you find out what she survived it's shocking, but it also makes a lot of sense. That grittiness didn't happen by chance. *Just sayin'.*

But when the first seizure happened I PANICKED big time. I immediately dropped a few hundred dollars on 8 different medical ID's bc I kept on buying them concurrently with my research as opposed to waiting until the end. So I spent a lot of money, but I sure felt

SAFE!! I also had a nice chat with my amazing Neurologist who pointed out that I had a very different type of injury and that if I were going to have a seizure it would have happened already. I felt a lot better after her reassurance. Still, I started wearing a Medical ID daily.

I had never worn one prior to 2016. It had honestly never occurred to me. Dr. Dogan (my surgeon) had saved my life and gotten 100% of the AVM out of my brain – my job was to deal with the ramifications. But there was no reason to think I'd have another episode. Still, when I mentioned my desire to start wearing a Medical ID to Boo Boo she said, *You know, I was actually thinking that might be a good idea.* I was shocked – she had never mentioned it. But I had been spending a couple months at a time at Boo Boo's house and it occurred to me that it made perfect sense. Wearing the right kind of Medical ID could really offer peace of mind to the people who are around me. If an incident happens there is enough to stress out about. Your family/friends are going to prioritize comforting YOU. It's very difficult to recall details about insurance and medicine dosages when under pressure.

So after buying all of those Medical ID's this is what I learned:
**note: I am not affiliated with any of these companies in any way. I'm just sharing my research.

(1) Basic
- A ton of online retailers allow you to customize basic Medical ID's
- A great choice if you can fit the relevant information into the character limits.
- E.g. people might just need to know: [Food] allergy | EPI pen in [location]
- ICE stands for "In Case of Emergency" – it is generally shorthand for your Emergency Contact Phone No. So you might add a line that says, ICE: Mom xxx-xxx-xxxx
- Completely healthy athletes might choose to wear a Medical ID, or a Road Runner ID, etc. in case something happens during an Iron Man or a race/ride and they collapse without their drivers license on them.

(2) Pretty
- Many of the "basic" options are actually pretty. You can get bracelets, necklaces, etc.
- Need more options: I like LaurensHope.com – very pretty things.
- I eventually chose a rose gold dog tag and I wear it with the Hope for Hankey tag I got engraved with Matt's logo from another retailer. Eventually I decided that a necklace was the best option for me, and a dog tag offered more room for my information.

(3) USB Drive ID

- Some ID's contain a USB drive on which you save vital medical information, including images as appropriate.
- I was not thrilled at the idea of the ID being damaged and the EMT having to plug it in to his/her laptop

(4) Online Profile

- I rely on MyID, sold by Endevr. Their tag line is, "Vital Information for Unthinkable Moments." They sell bracelets etc. with an 800 number and website (myidband.com or getmyid.com), plus a PIN linked to your personal profile. First responders are supposed to either call the phone number, go online to the public portal, or they can scan the QR code with their phone and gain instant access to your profile.
- The profile includes all your conditions, doctors, insurance, medications, and is maintained by you via an app you keep on your phone.
- In addition to medical jewelry, Endevr sells stickers with the contact info, PIN and QR code that you can affix to anything – e.g. a card you keep in your wallet, or your child's bike helmet.
- This app and the basic profile are free – it's actually really helpful for me when filling out paperwork. I don't have to remember everything – I just copy what I wrote down in the app.

- You can pay for a monthly subscription for a more robust online profile that allows you to store more information – relevant documents and images, e.g. if you have an active AVM sometimes people like to have their images readily available so the doctors know the exact location right away.
- Endevr sells several sporty bands, sleek ones, and several fashionably pretty choices. When I was in the market selection was more limited. So I ordered a clear sporty band and when it still got in my way too much I chose to have my PIN etc. engraved on a Laurens Hope dog tag.

The companies who sell Medical IDs that are designed to not look basic say that EMT's are trained to check you for tags and to recognize them even if they are disguised as pretty jewelry. I'm not sure what the reality of the situation is and hope to never find out. However, when I started wearing my tag I was glad to inform my people, *If anything happens, which it WON'T, tell the Medics to go to this website and enter my PIN. All the info is there.* This way, the person I'm with is free to concentrate on the task at hand – David and Randy think about Training. My friends think of laughing and eating. I keep an ID on the bannister at our garage door in case I'm in the house and am not wearing my ID – Mommy Daddy know exactly where to find one. I wear my steel tag daily, but if I'm going to be in the water at the gym I wear a silicone sports band from MYID. On days I didn't want to wear any jewelry – the noise was bothering me, or something – I dropped my tag on Randy's desk and told him it was there.

During the weekend after Megan's first seizure I was so stressed out my blood pressure (a known problem I am medicated for) was climbing rather alarmingly. In a last ditch attempt to feel better I emailed David and Randy saying, I'm not expecting this to happen, but in the event that I ever have to make a hasty exit from The Gym or The Clinic I *fully expect* you to ride in the ambulance with me. It worked – I sent that email and my BP immediately dropped 20 points.

It was peace of mind. I had a plan and had informed my people. That's why I wear a Medical ID in the first place. I'm all kinds of stable right now, but just in case anything ever happens there's a plan and I might not be able to speak for myself, but I've made provision for that and made my best effort to make relevant information available.

Ch. 13 We Can Hear You

WHAT TO DO WHEN SOMEONE YOU LOVE IS ASLEEP IN THE HOSPITAL

I will occasionally receive a message from an individual who has a loved one who's asleep in the hospital. Let's call the person who is awake "The Waiter." The Waiter is looking for something – *anything* to give them some insight into this horrible situation. There are so many moving parts here. No one can predict what's going to happen with 100% accuracy in every situation. But there is ONE THING you should know:

WE CAN HEAR YOU.

I speak from personal experience that is confirmed by a body of research. If you have a loved one who is asleep in the hospital, please assume that (s)he can hear everything you say, even if (s)he cannot communicate back. This includes the content of your speech as well as the tone of voice you use, and should influence

1. What you say
2. How you say it
3. How you permit Group Visits to unfold in your Loved One's presence

I cannot tell you whether or not your Loved One is going to wake up. I don't know. But what I am willing to state definitively is that

    A. I'm sorry this is happening

    B. "I love you," is always a good thing to say

When I got sick, word spread quickly. My friends called each other and tried to break the news gently. Joyce told me how she found out. She was running errands and suddenly her phone was lit up by multiple phone calls. *Uh oh. Not good* – she knew that if multiple people were calling her that something had happened.

She waited and answered the next call – it was Bob. (Bob and Joyce are my childhood friends from church). He was like, *Are you sitting down?*

> *Side Note: Ruthie made sure Ernie was sitting down and alone bc Ernie was in the office at the time. Boo Boo also knew something was wrong bc Mommy called her and left a voicemail. Mommy NEVER leaves voicemails. Justin called Randa (she and Joyce are sisters, but Randa had gotten married and moved away – but Justin remembered to call her asap) – thank you to everyone who made these difficult phone calls.*

I got sick in Oregon, but the friends I grew up with are in Maryland. My family booked the next flights to

PDX, and my friends were like, *What can we do?* Kim brought her laptop to church and made a video for me to watch as I woke up. Families and individuals recorded messages – some were tearjerkers, some were hilarious – all were full of love. But in the first few hours they did 2 things:

(1) They held an emergency prayer meeting. After MommyDaddy got the call from the ER doctor, Daddy sent out this message:

4.7.11

> *Dear All,*
>
> *We received a call from a doctor in an emergency room hospital in Portland, Oregon, at about 3 pm.*
> *Ning was found unconscious in a ladies room at Intel this morning. The doctor said Ning had a stroke and there appears to be massive bleeding. They have put her on a ventilator as she is not breathing on her own. They have transferred her to [OHSU].*
>
> *We are trying to get in touch with some believers in the W Assembly.*
>
> *We are trying to book air tickets to Portland.*
>
> *Ning had called home yesterday and informed she had a cold. She has been to her doctor for a physical recently and is reported to be in excellent health. This has come as a sudden shock to us.*
>
> *As you are aware, Ning had a few weeks ago returned from a trip to Burundi. She had no health issues when in Burundi.*
> *We shall deeply appreciate your prayers and the prayers of the saints to our Father of Mercies for Ning.*

Love in the Lord, Juio & P.T.

By 5 pm Dan Uncle sent out this message:

Jason K has suggested that we meet at the Chapel at 7.30 pm for prayer for Ning. I will be there. Anyone wishing to join may do so...

Many dear ones showed up and I have been told that the whole thing was..."rough." Thanks for praying for me, everyone xoxoxo.

(2) Since everybody couldn't get on a plane to Portland, they wrote me cards

My sweet friend Joycee asked our friends what *they* were going to write bc seriously? What are you SUPPOSED to say in a situation like this?

Bob's answer was short and sweet: *I just told her she HAS to get better. She has no choice* [insert emoji with slit eyes]

Franny: *Just remember – you don't know when your card is going to get there.*

Franny's advice was great – gently coded but to-the-point. In those early hours no one knew if I would live or die. Franny was simply saying that whatever you say, remember to make it appropriate for either outcome.

What a task!! All I can say is that my friends rose to the occasion.

As Franny pointed out, there are 2 basic possibilities here.

(A) The Person Wakes Up

The doctors cannot predict this with 100% accuracy, but they will tell you what they think based on their medical experience – the Waiter(s) will process this information and come to their own decision on how to handle this. I have Survivor Friends who were not expected to wake up, but did anyway – this will not always happen – but it can. In my own case the docs said, if she "responds" within 72 hours after surgery, she will eventually wake up. I responded just prior to the deadline but was still asleep for another month. The expectation was, however, that I would regain consciousness – this is how my family and friends prepared for my return to the Land of the Living:

Basically, If your Loved One wakes up, (s)he's gonna wake up SCARED. The Waiter's job is to mitigate this.

- **Explain**: Start explaining why they are in the hospital. Tell them the story of their injury again and again.
- **Use Visual Aids**: The nurses told my family to surround me with pictures that were familiar.

233

So my siblings gathered photos from my fridge and from around my apartment, duplicated them at Target, and made me a pretty picture board that traveled with me to all 3 hospitals. I stared at it all the time once I opened my eyes.

- **Leverage Music:** This goes back to how WE CAN HEAR YOU. Auditory memory is crazily strong.

  o When I met G, the nurse who got me to "respond" by pinching me, I had to pretend to be super cool and nonchalant but on the inside I was shaking like a leaf. I met her in 2014 when I returned to Oregon to dispose of my belongings. She had not seen me conscious. I was largely asleep when she cared for me in April 2011. But when she greeted me that morning 3 years later I stopped in my tracks – I KNEW HER VOICE.

  o I have no visual memory of June and J-P visiting me in Vibra (2nd hospital), but *I heard June's voice*. SNIFF. One day I sat in front of her at church and her singing voice caught me off guard – it made me think of those early days when I was so scared. Tears came to my eyes and tried desperately not to let them spill over. But yeah – I remembered her voice, too.

- o Talented singers sang to me in the hospital. I am a church musician, so these impromptu concerts were familiar and comforting. They also played me music to listen to. Music heals. Use it.
- **Make Your Presence Known:** The staff at every hospital knew that the level of care I received was expected to be the highest simply bc my Waiters made their presence known. They did this first (the ones local to Portland), by congregating in the waiting room during surgery. And eventually when I was downgraded to a unit that allowed visitors, they all came to see me. One of my docs asked a few years later, *SERIOUSLY?!?! Could you have ANY MORE friends?* She also informed me, *You had the best decorated room, EVER.* Your presence sends a signal – that you CARE. The patient needs to know this, but so does the staff.
- **Create Routine:** From the patient's perspective everything familiar is gone. The Waiter can bring comfort by establishing new hospital-based routines. Examples:
  - o My lips were SO chapped. When I gained the motor skills to point to my lips I knew that every time I did this Mommy would put Vaseline on them. (Thanks, Mommy).
  - o Every night Daddy would tell me a funny little "good night" poem that he used

to say when we were kids (Thanks, Mr. Dad)

After your Loved One goes through the scared phase it is very likely that (s)he will become angry like I did. Please see ch. 2 "Is it okay that you lived?"

(B) The Person Does Not Wake Up

This is not a scenario I can address with bullet points. I will simply point you to *Vol. 4 Learning How to Sing a New Song.* It was Carol Ridgely's dying wish for the world to know her story– I am so grateful that she let me tell it.

God saved her from a horrible life on the street. Christianity transformed her, but she still had to live in the body that had seen all those years of Bad Things. We became friends in 1998-'99 when I was a freshman at Georgetown University and she was at Georgetown Medical Center to get a new liver. The transplant didn't solve all her problems – the damage went way beyond the liver, plus there's all the drama associated with getting the body to accept a new organ in the first place.

One night she was silent with pain – she literally had nothing left in the tank with which to produce a scream. *Please, Ning,* she pleaded in a whisper, I can't take anymore. *Pray me home.*

I burst into tears. I was 18 or 19. I had lived a very comfortable and sheltered life. I was NOT prepared to pray Mrs. Ridgely home.

I forgot that story – she told it to me over a decade later after I got sick. And when she was diagnosed with a terminal cancer in 2015 on top of everything else, I knew that it was time. So I asked myself the question, What does it mean to walk with someone until the very end?

There are some very complicated questions here, and I am not prepared to deal with all of them. However, I will offer these thoughts –

CHILDREN:

If there are children involved, they are your priority. The Rule is simple: **Protect the Children**. It's like Marlene's rule from the Intro – if you fall, HANDS off the STROLLER. Your job is to keep the baby safe. If there are children involved in the situation, remember that they are *children* – they should not be exposed to too much, too soon. If they visit with the Asleep person, please ensure that you try to make the child feel as safe as possible, e.g. hold hands, let the kid sit in your lap and talk to the person, etc. If the child indicates to you that it is too stressful, (s)he is too sad/scared, that's totally okay. Offer to convey a message to the person who is asleep. Take a break and visit the hospital vending machine or gift shop.

Better yet, do what my family did, and take the kids to a park or something. I know it sounds weird, but when ERKE(P) (there was no P2 yet) came to see me in the 2nd hospital I had all sorts of dreams about them bc on some level I knew they were there even though my eyes weren't open. But a few years later when I saw all the pics and vids they took of their visit I actually got jealous – I had missed out on all the family time bc I was asleep.

Ernie and Ruth had flown across the country with a 5-year old and an 18-month old to visit me. They knew it was important for us to be together. But they also made sure that the kids got enough play time and break time. A lovely lady from my church invited the entire family over for Easter lunch and they staged an egg hunt in her home. (Ruth had brought the plastic eggs with her.) They somehow maintained a sense of normalcy in a very abnormal situation.

I received several visits from children (with their parents) as I began to wake up. And I learned how to care for the sick as a child – Mommy took me everywhere with her. But I did not engage with death until I was older. Sometimes it's unavoidable – no one knows how old a kid is going to be when (s)he has to say goodbye to someone they love. But the point is, please be attentive to these young ones – some will plant themselves in the middle of action and handle the situation with wisdom way beyond their years – they will be the ones to comfort everyone else. But other children will need you to be on the lookout for signs of distress – they might not be able to verbalize their trouble, but please just scoop them up and give them a hug.

DO YOU FEEL UNPREPARED FOR THIS?

In 2005 I had the Very High Honor of watching for 3 days at Aunty Sila's bedside while she waited to die. And yes, I was *literally* at her bedside. I arrived for a visit a couple days before Christmas, gauged the situation, and never left. I slept on the twin bed next to hers. Well, there wasn't a whole lot of sleeping. I talked to her. She had an extremely bad cancer and Uncle Bill had brought her home from hospice care bc she had previously informed him that she wanted to die in her own home. As you know, I am not a medical professional. And as I cared for Aunty Sila I'd apologize and tell her how sorry I was that I was so clumsy.

Day 2 got better bc Bob came over to help!! He distracted Uncle Bill with his iPod, I made Uncle Bill coffee and did laundry, and at night when Aunty Sila needed to take meds Bob and I lifted her while Uncle Bill tried to coax the pills down her throat. It was largely a fruitless effort, however, bc she had refused to ingest anything for 48 hours.

If you know us, Bob and I are NOT the A-Team if you are assembling hospice caregivers. That is an understatement. If anyone had a reason to feel inadequate, we did. But we were there for one reason: **We loved her.**

Actually, there was another reason: We loved Uncle Bill, too.

Of *course* you feel unprepared for this. *Everyone* does. But you're there for a reason and it's the one and only credential you need: LOVE.

Ch. 14 Champion

THERE'S A CHAMPION INSIDE ALL OF US.

...

CHAMPIONS OVERCOME.

BAHAHAHAHA!!

Sorry – it's naughty to laugh like that, but I can't help it. Trainer David seriously says stuff like this with a completely straight face during tense Training moments. He knows that The Valley gave me a different perspective on life and the majority of his Motivational Speeches don't work on me. So he intentionally plays them up to make me laugh. Laughing is always a good idea in my world.

Or else he will just be mean or extremely matter of fact.

Examples:

Are you going to stand there, or are you gonna SQUAT?!?! (we have some of our finest moments while bickering in the squat rack.)

I hear a whole lot of whimpering, but I don't feel any breathing. YOU'D BETTER START BREATHING. (he was fixing my shoulder and I was holding my breath/writhing/curling up into a ball and trying to roll away)

D: [Early in Training, D brings a humongous kettlebell out] I just need one rep. It's going to FEEL like it's not going to move, but it WILL, I promise.
Me: Ummm....THAT's your pep talk?

I like to give him a hard time. At first it was an indirect signal to him that I was afraid, but now I do it just for fun. I fully understand that he is in charge and plan on eventually do what he tells me to do, but I think it makes his work day more interesting if we "discuss" things first. And D provides A LOT of material for discussion. David's motivational style is very verbal, whereas Randy's is eerily quiet. To be clear, Randy is a very nice person – I don't think he's doing it on purpose. But the overall effect is...[blinks]....yes, Sensei.

There are TV screens all over the clinic and one day Randy and I paused at the end of the agility ladder to watch a young woman win gold at the RIO Olympics (2016). She is from our area and Randy trained her back in the day. A couple of us were standing there and Randy remarked to someone else,

She was one of the only athletes who really "got it." The only others who were like that were [he named 2 people]. They'd ask, "Am I doing this right?" And,

"How can I do this better?" They really wanted to know – they listened, and then they did it.

I reflected deeply on this statement and filed it away for our next book. I would consider the 2 athletes Randy named to be big deals in American Sport. It's significant that even *I* know who they are – and their names immediately summoned certain iconic images/photographs in my mind. And then I consulted Google, who confirmed that yes, these athletes *also* brought home Olympic gold.

Hmmmmm....I think Randall just verbalized how to be a champion.

When I first started writing in public I named everything, "Learning How." My blog, books, and website all bore this name, and when Daddy did the legal work to form a company for me we called it, "Learning How – a Non Profit Corporation." It took me 2 seconds to come up with "Learning How." I knew from the get go that I had no idea how to live This Disabled Life so I just decided to chronicle my adventures in Learning How to do this. I started writing at the end of 2012 – the start of 2013. Five years have gone by and I've learned A LOT.

Recently I unearthed the prayer journal I used the year prior to my injury. My church found it amongst my belongings and mailed it to me (thank you!). I looked at it for the first time a month ago and it proves that yeah, I have learned a lot in Recoveryland – but all these lessons were built on the foundation laid prior to the bleed. During that time I was very much in a "Learning How" mindset. I resolved within myself to find strength in solitude (I had started a new life in a new city), and to have a Teachable Spirit that could observe and emulate the life-patterns of certain high-impact individuals who took the time to show me how to participate in the Divine.

Actually, the fact that I had moved from the D.C. area to Oregon was highly calculated on my part. It was my way of making a grand gesture of "availability." I wrote this in my prayer journal:

Q: *What kind of person do I want to be?*

A: *The kind of person God can use.*

And I wrote further that *If I won't even move to Oregon – where there's a job waiting for me and I already know people* (I had interned the summer before and received a full-time offer), HOW could God ever send me anywhere else? So moving to Oregon was my way of practicing saying, "Yes" to God and indicating that I was open to whatever He planned for my future.

When I wanted to become a missionary and believed that God was calling me to Africa I devoted myself to praying for a new Life's work, did some hardcore building of strong spiritual practices (prayer, reading, fasting), looked for opportunities to serve (e.g. housecleaning) and learn new skills (e.g. teaching ESL, church A/V team), attached myself to older and wiser warriors in faith who could teach me what to do, and begged God to show me if I were wrong in thinking He was calling me to the Third World. I did what I had in front of me to the best of my ability and did some vigorous searching on how I could raise my level of play. I was proceeding in good faith and believed my heart was pure as I sought His will, and that He would show me if I were misunderstanding where He was leading me.

Step-by-step I went through the forms of decision-making based on a fervent desire to know and do what He wanted me to do.

And then I woke up in the hospital with a month of my life missing, and my independence, my financial security, and my future plans GONE.

I was horrified. When I first told Daddy I wanted to go to Africa he had told me, *We have to be very careful about this and will pray about it quietly for a while. Because if we move too fast, and it turns out you're wrong, your faith will be extremely damaged.*

Daddy was right. We did not move fast – I spent 6 months praying silently about my desire go to Africa before I mentioned it to anyone bc I thought I might be crazy. And then once I realized that it was not a passing fancy and told Daddy, we spent several MORE months in silent prayer. In the end I was thrilled to have the support of my family and both of my churches as my path seemed to be leading clearly across the Atlantic. Then when God put me in a wheelchair instead of allowing me to join the King's Service overseas I was *so* sad. Okay, not just sad, *mad*. White-hot angry, in fact.

But because He kept me cognitively intact I had a lot of time to think while I was bedridden but awake. And eventually (by using simple logic) I decided that *Yes, I've had hearing loss – but I can STILL hear the Shepherd's voice.*

He's not trying to trick me. I'm asking in earnest to be led in the right direction and counting on the verse, *If any of you lack wisdom, let him ask of God, that giveth to all men liberally, and upbraideth not; and it shall be given him. James 1.5*

As I came to terms with what happened I had to admit that although I was aghast at this turn of events I could not claim to have been unprepared. Because I *was* – 110% prepared for this, the role of my life. Eventually I came to understand that although I was specifically trained for this life through education and personal/professional experience, no one is strictly necessary in God's plan. He just gives us an opportunity to participate in a miracle sometimes.

No one's going to dispute the idea that it's pretty fantastic to participate in a miracle. And although my original entry into this situation was NOT my choice, I *did* have plenty of opportunity to plan my response. You can imagine that if I had come to a different conclusion on Decision Day (see ch. 2) I would have been equally vocal about it. But once I realized the magnitude of the opportunity that He had given me - that I would be given the gift of healing and that I'd get to talk about it, I jumped in with both feet.

(Side note: Figuratively, of course. I don't jump unless David or Randy makes me.)

The foundation God had laid prior to my bleed was exactly what I needed once I got sick. I have full documentation on this (my old prayer journals). But please don't ask to see them bc I'm still weirded out by the whole thing and have hidden the journals in my closet. For real, though, I like proof, proof, and MORE proof. I did not believe them when they said I had a brain injury. I learned the hard way that I could not walk. (Sorry, Andrew aka PT2 – *my bad.*)

But as I have searched those prayer journals as life has become even more complicated and I've recovered enough to be able to handle more, one thing is crystal clear: I was called to trust God in completely radical ways prior to my illness, and the way I live now is simply an extension of that.

Most of the time, insight into what I should do and how I should do it has been given to me via the people God gave me to help me heal. When I began Recovery I immediately recognized that this is not my area of expertise. I have zero medical background and biology class really grossed me out. So I made it a point to learn everything I could from my Therapists, and when I had the opportunity, to surround myself with gifted people who could teach me how to live.

When Randy joined the Team I wrote on my blog, "There are no benchers or subs on Team Tanimal. If you are here, plan on working hard. We're playing for keeps and I will extract *every ounce* of expertise from you. I have ways and means..." (Learning How – blog post "Team Tanimal" – 3.12.14)

I made it my priority to recognize and recruit talent. And I'm so grateful for everything they've taught me – to work a wheelchair, to stand, sit, eat, run, breathe, use my eyes and my voice....it's been quite the learning process.

But I can answer some questions, the hardest ones like, *Why is this happening,* or *HOW am I supposed to respond to this situation?* only through the lens of my faith – so sorry, it's not fully transferable, but it's still interesting, so I'm going to tell you about it.

One of my favorite books is *The Hiding Place*, by Corrie Ten Boom. She was a middle-aged watchmaker when she became a leader in the Dutch Resistance in Nazi-occupied Holland during WWII. She and her family were eventually incarcerated for hiding Jews in a secret room they had built in their house. You can still see it today if you go to Haarlem, Holland – the Beje is a museum now.

Corrie's lovely sister, Betsy, was one of the Ten Booms who died in a concentration camp. And on the day they arrived at Ravensbruck (I think), the sisters stood outside of their new barracks and could see even from far away that the building was crawling with filth. (Side note: they had been incarcerated in another facility and had survived a couple of horrifying train rides and snow marches, so they were not uninitiated in the ways of camp life. But this was a new level of degradation.)

Corrie: *Lord, we cannot live here. You CANNOT expect this of us.*

Betsy: *Show us how, Lord, **show us how.***

Corrie writes that she heard Betsy ask for help out loud and realized that as her sister got closer to eternity the line between prayer and "real life" got increasingly blurred. (Side note – it turns out that the barracks were SO FILTHY that even the guards refused to go near the building. So the women who lived there met with a level of unexpected freedom in that environment.)

The line of demarcation between prayer and life is definitely blurred for me, and I wouldn't have it any other way. I've learned a lot and been given so much help, but for the toughest stuff of life I have no alternative but to ask, *Show me how, Lord. Show me how to do this.*

And you know what? It's worked well enough for me to have a ton of evidence (bc yes, I have documented this entire process) that tells me that I have enough reason to keep on hoping and trusting that the next step will be shown to me at the right time.

There is no question in anyone's mind when they see me that this method (my faith) works. That said, none of the people I interact with today have a first-hand knowledge of what happened. No one on this side of the country was an eyewitness to the onset of my injury.

Summary: it was bad. I tried to trick Dr. Dogan (the surgeon who saved my life) into re-stating the severity of my situation when I saw him in 2014 – 3 years after my craniectomy on April 7, 2011. I had already decided that I would scrupulously avoid any questions regarding prognosis (since I already knew that I wouldn't believe him, anyway, bc I don't believe ANYONE), but for some reason I had it in my head that my future would be more hopeful if I could get him to say that what happened to me wasn't so bad after all.

I put out multiple verbal fishing hooks. He didn't bite. Not ONCE. And when I tried the same trick on the Doctor on call at the time of my surgery (then a Resident), she stuck to her story, too. It was Bad. VERY. BAD. Blood was everywhere (internally – they vacuumed it out). I was almost dead by the time they scraped me off the floor at work and I eventually made it onto his table. I was "sooooo close." (This was accompanied by expressive hand gestures.)

So when no one was going along with my "it wasn't so bad" story, I gave up on finding renewed hope during that visit. But then Dr. Dogan surprised me with a statement that was not based on his medical experience – it came straight from the heart.

He looked at me and based on what he saw, he shed the Surgeon persona and just talked to me like a person. Given the state I had been in on the day of surgery contrasted with the Me of three years later, it was definitely an extraordinary case. He only had one student with him that day, but I think I ruined the teaching moment. However, I provided a good example of the better than best-case scenario – the kind of outcome no one anticipates.

I was standing up to show him that I *could* stand, that I was building core strength, etc, I told him how I had just gotten a Personal Trainer and an Athletic Trainer, and that I was going to learn how to run. He looked at me, and then glanced down at the book I had brought him (a copy of *Volume 1*). He looked back up at me again and it was like time froze. It was a time-out from the usual exam-room doctor talk. He just said, *In the future when you have to make a decision, DO NOT HESITATE. It's going to be the right one.*

Dr. Dogan actually knows very little about me. He made this statement based on the extent of Recovery he saw. And he's seen a lot of cases, FYI. He teaches people how to do this (life-saving brain surgery, etc.). I was just a patient he operated on in April 2011. And then I popped up in his landscape again 3 years later.

During that trip to Oregon I visited all 3 of my hospitals and the look I saw in so many eyes was nothing less than *hunger*. The doctors, nurses, and Therapists all scrutinized my physical condition with almost fierce intensity. I took special care in my extensive grooming routine and tried hard to stand up straight – LOL. I expected to be looked at a lot. After all, I am their handiwork – I'm proof that they are good at what they do. There was more than one jaw on the ground when I called them by name and said, *It's me, Ning – do you remember?*

Yeah, they remembered.

I saw a lot of people during that trip (and I shed a lot of tears in private). Those people were the ones who were kind to me when I woke up and was confused. When I couldn't communicate, they were the ones to take care of me even though I couldn't say what I needed.

But seeing my surgeon was the highlight of my hospital visitation schedule. He didn't really know me – he did his job on Day 1 and I wasn't there to ask for anything more. Hey, Dr. Dogan: 2 Things –

1. Thanks for saving my life. Sorry I was really ungrateful at first (I saw him 3 mo. after surgery and thanked him only because Daddy said I had to).
2. Thank you for your vote of confidence.

In the years since I saw Dr. Dogan in 2014 I have thought about what he said to me, especially when I have had reason to doubt myself. Essentially, he gave me his vote of confidence that day. He ascertained that something "different" was going on with my situation that could reasonably be expected to carry through to the rest of my life. And at this point in my Recovery I can say that I feel very confident in all of the choices I've made.

Every single choice has been based on the premise that I'm proceeding in good faith, and that if I'm making a mistake, God will show me. It's the

Teachable Spirit in a scarily high-stakes scenario. I always want to know if I'm doing this (Life) right, and how I can improve on it.

The paper trail shows that I have spent a good decade cultivating this attitude, and now it's show time. So I'm going to keep on asking how to do this better, and what I DO know how to do, I plan on doing enthusiastically. This is the kind of mindset that produces Champions.

Made in the USA
Columbia, SC
01 March 2018